Praise for **Buyer**

"Carole Mahoney's innovative, research-based methods will revolutionize the way you think about sales, connect with buyers, and grow your business. Say goodbye to outdated tactics and read this book instead."

DANIEL H. PINK, #1 *New York Times*–bestselling author of *To Sell Is Human*, *Drive*, and *When*

"An essential resource for business owners, entrepreneurs, and sellers to demystify sales success through actionable research and data that transforms personal sales results."

MARK ROBERGE, author of *The Sales Acceleration Formula* and senior lecturer at Harvard Business School

"Finally, a sales book for business owners and salespeople that digs into the hidden weaknesses in sales execution that no one is talking about. This book is a paradigm shift on how to think about selling, the buying process, and human connection. Reading *Buyer First* will not only make you a better salesperson but a better person."

MELINDA F. EMERSON, author of *Become Your Own Boss in 12 Months*

"Mindset, strategies, and a clear path to competitive advantage—this book has it all. Carole Mahoney has done the impossible: written the sales book that has never been written before, and one that is long overdue. *Buyer First* is packed with powerful research, engaging stories, and real-life tactics on what it takes to excel in sales today—confidence, action, results! If you're in sales, read it; if you lead a sales team, share it; and if you want to help anyone take their sales game to the next level, buy it!"

MERIDITH ELLIOTT POWELL, author of *Thrive*

"While 'buyer first' is an essential concept in business today, Carole Mahoney has created an entire ecosystem for your sales processes. From concept, to origin story, to mindset blocks, to effective strategies, it's all here for sustainable success in sales. A book you will refer back to time and time again."

JEFFREY SHAW, author of *The Self-Employed Life* and *Lingo*

"*Buyer First* is a needed guide for salespeople today. It's not enough to know what you need to do. You must do it. Carole Mahoney will help you recognize why you aren't doing what you know you need to do and inspire you to *act now*!"

ANTHONY IANNARINO, author of *Elite Sales Strategies*

"Packed with powerful sales strategies that are backed by real scientific studies, *Buyer First* is a book you need to read. Carole Mahoney's in-depth understanding of what today's buyers want and need when making buying decisions guides every chapter of this well-written book. The exercises throughout will also help you implement what you learn, which will enable you to better serve buyers and earn more sales."

DAVID HOFFELD, chief sales trainer at Hoffeld Group and bestselling author of *The Science of Selling*

"When you master the mindsets Carole Mahoney details in *Buyer First*, you will be able to adapt to the ever-changing economic circumstances and buying behaviors we see today. Rather than a process to memorize or tricks to try, this book gives you the insights and tools to engage with buyers in the ways that they value most."

DAVE KURLAN, author of *Baseline Selling* and founder of Objective Management Group

"Sales is a discouraging process for many, but it doesn't have to be. *Buyer First* is an actionable guide to elevate your 'game' and your comfort."

MIKE MICHALOWICZ, author of *Profit First*, *Clockwork*, and *All In*

"Carole Mahoney smashes the typical sales stereotypes with data, science, and real-world experiences. When you read *Buyer First* and do the exercises, not only will you change how you think about sales, you will also change how your buyers see you and your solution. You may find that you enjoy sales without being 'salesy.'"

ANDY PAUL, author of *Sell without Selling Out*

"*Buyer First* is a must-read for those who understand that the nature of the relationship between buyers and sellers has fundamentally changed. Want to increase your sales? Imagine a strategy as simple as putting your buyer's needs first. Sounds good? The challenge is, while many executives claim to be customer-focused, most of their customers would disagree. Not only does Carole Mahoney share why this is, and what this looks like in your role, but she also guides you in changing your mindset and skills for you to succeed by putting your buyers first."

BRYAN EISENBERG, coauthor of *Waiting for Your Cat to Bark?* and *The Rice & Beans Millionaire*

"Being an entrepreneur is hard enough without making it harder with old-school sales tactics. The days of the pushy, slimy salesperson are numbered. *Buyer First* will change your sales game in a way that makes you stick out as a reliable resource for your buyers. They will thank you for it!"

(JIM) KEENAN, author of *Gap Selling*

"*Buyer First* is a very smart read for any entrepreneur or new business owner wanting to understand the art and science of selling. It is also a top suggested read for the sales professional who is stuck in a rut, or starting new, to help them break unsupportive habits and move into more success."

LORI RICHARDSON, author of *She Sells*

BUYER FIRST

Grow Your Business with Collaborative Selling

CAROLE MAHONEY

BUYER FIRST

PAGE TWO

For my boys—Steve, Nate, MJ, and Loki

Some names and identifying details have been changed to protect the privacy of individuals.

Cataloguing in publication information is available from Library and Archives Canada.
ISBN 978-1-77458-320-3 (paperback)
ISBN 978-1-77458-321-0 (ebook)

Page Two
pagetwo.com

Edited by James Harbeck
Copyedited by Melissa Edwards
Proofread by Alison Strobel
Cover and interior design by Fiona Lee
Cover illustration by Michelle Clement
Printed and bound in Canada by Friesens
Distributed in Canada by Raincoast Books
Distributed in the US and internationally by Macmillan

23 24 25 26 27 5 4 3 2 1

carolemahoney.com

CONTENTS

INTRODUCTION

Remember that just because you hit rock bottom doesn't mean you have to stay there.
ROBERT DOWNEY JR.

"I'M SORRY MA'AM, it says your card has been declined."

The heat rose in my face. I looked at the items in my cart, all bagged up and ready to go, and then at the line of people behind me, and I stopped breathing.

It wasn't supposed to be like this. Going into business for myself was supposed to mean freedom, not this.

That night, as I was lying in bed next to my husband, the scene in the grocery store played over and over in my head as I stared at the ceiling. I needed to sleep so I could get up early for my networking meeting the next day. I had to be on my game; I had to get some clients in soon, so I—

Steve rolled over and whispered, "You need to shut your brain off. I can hear it from over here."

The floodgates opened. "How am I going to buy presents for the kids?" I cried through mucus-filled hiccups. "What mother can't buy groceries and Christmas presents for her kids?"

"I can buy presents for the boys. Stop worrying about it—they are my stepsons now. And everyone has ups and downs, right?"

"Yes, but it's been six months since I brought any money in. How did I get here? Maybe everyone is right—I'm not cut out for this, and I should go find a job."

Weeks later, I found myself staring at the blinking cursor on my Word document. I had to get this blog post finished; I had not published anything in months—no wonder I didn't have any new clients. But what could I write about that wouldn't make me feel like a complete fraud in that moment? How could I tell people how to get more business when I couldn't do it for myself?

Maybe Steve is right. This is just a down time. Plenty of business owners work a job and do their own thing on the side. The economy is turning around, more people are hiring, and I must provide for my family. This crazy idea that I can be my own boss and design my life the way I want will have to wait.

After several weeks of searches, applications, and interviews, my sister Heidi introduced me to her boss, who was looking for a content marketing director. Because Jack knew my sister, he was very candid with me and shared that the role was between me and one other person, who happened to be a man I knew—let's call him Frank.

"I don't know who to choose," he told me. "If you were me, what would you do?"

"What is the most important aspect of this role for you right now?" I asked.

"We do a lot of sporting events management and marketing. This person would need to be comfortable working with the administrative staff of several event venues and going to all the games."

I sighed. I guess I could do that. If I must.

"Well… as much as I would love to take the job, I know that Frank has done that before and loves it, whereas I have not. If I were you, I would hire him."

"Wow," he said. "I didn't expect that answer."

"I know, I must be crazy," I replied. "Here I am turning down a comfortable job that's local. But I believe Frank is a better fit for what you need, and I wouldn't want to put you, Heidi, or me in a position where we regretted the decision. I can find another opportunity that is a better fit."

"Please let me know how I can help," Jack said. "I appreciate your honesty and helping me figure this out. You made this decision a lot easier. I'm going to ask around to see who might need your services."

That was a surprise. No one had offered to do that before. If only every interview or sales conversation went that way!

What was different about this conversation from every other interview or conversation with a potential client?

It took me some time to realize: I wasn't trying to sell him on what I wanted and needed. Instead, I had put his needs ahead of my own. When I shared this thought with Steve, he said, "Maybe you need to stop trying to sell people in order to get more clients."

Sell without Selling

How do you sell people without selling them?

The answer to that question took me several more years to understand. I had to start all over again in my business before I started to see that selling isn't something we do *to* others; it is something we do *with* them. When we make selling all about us—what we do and what we need—sales becomes something we do to other people to get what we want. When we make selling about others' wants and needs, when we actively adopt a buyer first mindset, then sales becomes something we do with them.

Not only will you see better sales and business results when you adopt a buyer first mindset, you will become a better human too. When you focus your intentions to be not about you, you can free yourself from the fear of rejection and the need for others' approval and become more fully present in the here and now.

When I went through this process for myself, and then with my clients, it changed us. You as well must be ready, willing, and able to change to sell successfully with your buyers.

This is the book I wish I had nearly twenty years ago when I first started my business. While I am neither a therapist nor an academic scientist, I am intensely curious. Why do people do what they do? Why don't people do the things they know they should? How is it that some can overcome impossible odds, while others who have every opportunity throw it away?

This book is based on my own experience and on the experiences and results of my coaching clients. It includes decades of psychological research on how we change our mindsets and behaviors, coupled with data from over two million sales professionals on what it takes to be successful in sales without being, as Daniel Pink writes in *To Sell Is Human*, "pushy, slimy, or sleazy." This book is the result of a scientific process that started with what I have observed in myself and my clients, and asking the questions to understand why things are that way.

But I'm not a scientist, nor do you need to be one to understand and apply these principles. When you read this book and do the exercises, no matter how silly they may seem to you, you will know how to change your mindset toward sales so you can be more collaborative with your buyers, which is what they need in order to buy from you.

Sales is not something you do *to* other people, it is something you do *with* them. Embrace that mindset and you may find your next favorite client by the time you finish the last chapter. You may even find that your personal relationships have shifted.

Sales is not
something you do
to other people,
it is something you
do *with* them.

Good Luck—or Not

I hope that your situation is not as desperate as mine was back in 2008, six months after I started my business in the middle of the Great Recession. Maybe you believed that rejecting the corporate world is about gaining the freedom to control your own destiny—a risk you thought worth taking because there is no such thing as job security anymore. Maybe you believed, as I once did, that what you are offering is such a no-brainer that it would sell itself to your prospects. Or maybe, like many of my coaching clients who stumbled or chose to go into sales, you thought that this life would mean control over your income, because you had the power to directly impact your outcomes.

Sure, you knew it would not be easy. But did you know how much it would mess with your head? How it would leave your heart racing when the only thing you want to do is sleep? How it would put stress on your family and loved ones as they watch you struggle, or try to stay out of your way? Have you been wondering if you are cursed with bad luck?

I can tell you about luck. I grew up in a superstitious Irish family.

On a recent Friday the 13th, after I did my morning yoga on the deck in our backyard, I found myself reflecting on luck. With the eagles flying overhead and the air alive with the song of birds in spring, I thought about my clients' typical reaction to my outdoor office background—in the middle of the woods, overlooking a small lake in Maine. How lucky I must be! I laughed and thought about all I had gone through to get here.

Luck had next to nothing to do with it.

If I was lucky, I was lucky on purpose.

After I had been fired in the middle of a recession, starting a business seemed to be my only option. But with no savings, few contacts, two kids, and two mortgages, the odds were stacked against me. Luck was not on my side.

Then our tenants stopped paying their rent because, like me, they had been laid off. Then the banks never responded to the short sale they initially agreed to. And then—foreclosure.

To rebound from all that, I had to face up to some things, and fast: my own mindsets toward sales, my discomfort with discussing money, and my need for approval, to name a few. (Not to mention cancer and other health issues—more on that later.)

When I started to change those mindsets—and, ultimately, myself—my circumstances started to change with them. With that change came new behaviors that would lead to outcomes I could only have dreamed of.

Today, my steady six-figure income supports my family and allowed my husband to take a 50 percent pay cut in order to do what he enjoys. It allows us to travel when we want to, renovate our lakeside home, get off the grid, and invest in our family's future.

Wherever you are at now, in your business or your sales career, know this: You are the author of your story. You decide where your luck comes from.

Yes, there are parts that are hard and scary. Bravery comes when we don't hide from the challenges. My hope is that, when you read and do the exercises in this book, you will know what is getting in your way of your sales success, how to change it, and what to do with your buyers to apply it.

I invite you to lean into the fear and build your bravery. As you work through the exercises in this book, or when you have an "aha" moment, share it on social media with the hashtags #buyerfirst and #notaboutme (and tag me if you want). Show your work. Share your lessons and wins.

You've got this.

F**k luck.

1

YOU ARE A SALESPERSON

Everything is selling... Nothing happens in this world, nothing comes into this world, until somebody makes a sale... You don't believe me?... Where the hell do you think you'd be if your father hadn't sold your mother a bill of goods?

RICHARD YATES

YOU CAN'T ESCAPE the fact that you are a seller. As a business owner, you are in sales whenever you try to motivate team members, convince the bank to give you a loan, or negotiate with partners.

The same goes for your team members. They are in sales whenever they share their ideas or make the case for resources to implement them.

It applies to the two-year-old who never stops asking why, or never gives up when they want something. Just as it does for the parent trying to get them to eat their veggies or go to bed.

We are all selling something every day. As a business owner, you are selling yourself and your vision of the future. And as a salesperson—well, you get it.

Which means you have been selling your entire life.

Regardless of whether you are a business owner, entrepreneur, or salesperson in a company, the one thing you don't want to be called is *salesy*. Clients say it to me all the time: "I want to get more clients and customers, but I don't want to be salesy." Reconciling the image you have of yourself to include being a salesperson may feel uncomfortable at first. Somewhere in your mind you know it's true, but, as I did once, maybe you hope that you can find some way around it.

When I first started my marketing agency in 2007, right after getting laid off from my corporate job at the height of the Great Recession, I didn't simply want to avoid sales—I wanted to replace the need for sales altogether. Between my childhood experiences with salespeople—more on that soon—and my adult experiences with salespeople in the corporate world, my disdain was so strong that I wanted to make them obsolete. I believed that the internet was going to make that easy. Soon, anyone would be able to buy anything online, and the "pushy, slimy, sleazy" salesperson was an unnecessary middleman to be eliminated.

My bias was confirmed when I started getting my first client referrals from other agencies. Because I understood early how to use Google Analytics, leverage search engine optimization (SEO), and run pay-per-click campaigns, the traditional agencies wanted to subcontract me to clients who were asking for these new tactics. The recession was leading to slashed budgets, and strategies like the Yellow Pages and direct mail had become too expensive for the returns they offered.

Only six months after getting laid off from my former job, I was able to replace my lost salary and had the freedom to take my kids to school and pick them up every day. I thought I had it all figured out. I had started a business in the worst economic times and did it without ever having to sell anything myself. *I don't know why everyone said this would be so hard!* I thought.

I said no to a job offer, spent my entire first consulting check, and decided I must be way smarter than everyone else.

Psychologists call this Mount Stupid, or the Dunning-Kruger Effect. The less experience we have with a subject, the more likely we are to overestimate our strengths and underestimate our weaknesses in that subject. This is due not to arrogance but to ignorance. And it's not because we know we are lying to ourselves—we *believe* what we think. I believed I had it figured out and was well on my way to financial freedom—without having to make a single sales call.

But not long after that, those agency partners who had contracted me to work with their clients started to reduce my scope or cut me out of their proposals altogether to keep more work for themselves. Suddenly I found myself with no work, no contacts, and no savings. Now what?

I hired a business coach to help me figure it out. He told me right off that I needed to do some networking, read sales books, and invest in some sales training and workshops. I hated it, but I was desperate to do whatever it took to save my dreams.

I studied SPIN Selling, Solution Selling, Sandler Selling, Question Based Selling, Baseline Selling, Referral and Relationship selling, and any other new sales methodology that promised me results. If sales books were weight-loss programs, then I was the Oprah Winfrey of sales programs.

I tried anything and everything, failed at most of it, and hated all of it.

Perhaps you too have begrudgingly accepted that you need to get better at sales, and, as many do, you have chased after the latest trends, hoping that any given one will be the thing that unlocks success for you. That somehow knowing which transformational words to say, what mythical step-by-step process to follow, or which magical technology to use is the key to unlocking your elusive success.

That magic key does not yet exist, nor did it ever. There is no one-size-fits-all technique, word, or process that will bring you overnight sales success. But when you design a process for yourself that centers on your ideal client's buying process as well as your own unique strengths, tendencies, and areas where you need to improve, you can achieve consistent results, find new opportunities, reach your goals, and, beyond that, believe you can achieve bigger goals.

Sales? Ugh

In 2021, I decided to take on a survey of thirty-nine business owners to find out what their biggest needs were. I asked questions like what their biggest challenges have been since they started their business and what lead generation activities they were active in. Across those business owners, more than 90 percent stated that their biggest business challenge was getting new clients, yet 95 percent had checked off every box in the list of possible ways to find new clients. These initial results were confirmed by the Kauffman Foundation, which found that, during the pandemic, securing new customers was the number one challenge for 80 percent of business owners. And among business owners who had been in operation for more than ten years, that figure was still as high as 69 percent! From cold calling to social selling, business owners and sellers today are trying everything to get new clients and customers, yet not seeing the results they need to pay their bills and reach their goals.

Why?

Our mindset about sales is one big reason. It prevents us from being collaborative with our prospective buyers. Instead, we try every tip, tactic, or technology, only to get limited or no results. It is about what we do, as well as *how* we do it. We can learn the foolproof process, memorize the exact right words, and know all the right people, but if we are not able to execute on what we know we need to do in the moment we should do it, we will continue to get more of the same.

How do you change a mindset? The first step to change is to develop your awareness—of the existence of the mindsets holding you back, and of their root causes.

Think for a moment about your mindset toward sales. When you were asked as a kid what you wanted to be when you grew up, what did you say? Was it a salesperson? When I am giving a keynote or workshop and I ask my audience that question, I get some interesting looks. Some wince as if they had smelled last week's trash; others scowl like they had been insulted. Remember that stereotypical salesperson that Daniel Pink describes? Pushy. Slimy. Sleazy. Not only do most of us dislike sales and sellers and therefore not trust them, salespeople don't trust other salespeople! A study done by the sales assessment company Objective Management Group (OMG)—which produced much of the data I will present throughout this book—suggests that salespeople are equally as likely to distrust other salespeople as the rest of us. No wonder so few kids aspire to become a salesperson! Or why, as business owners, we resist the idea that we are in sales.

But it was that very mindset that caused my first business to fail. In fact, I might argue, it is this mindset toward sales that causes so many small and startup businesses to give up. Writing in *Entrepreneur,* Timothy Carter cites data from the U.S. Bureau of Labor Statistics showing that about 20 percent of small businesses fail within the first year. By the end of their fifth year, roughly half have faltered. After ten years, nearly 70 percent are gone.

And while several factors contribute to that failure rate, we can't ignore the biggest one. According to a 2020 working

The first step to change is to develop your awareness—
of the existence of the mindsets holding you back, and of their root causes.

paper from Tina Highfill of the U.S. Bureau of Economic Analysis and her research team, "almost 90 percent [of self-employed business owners] reported net income less than $50,000." Hardly enough money to justify the amount of time we spend and stress we have. But because of our attitudes and mindsets toward sales, we don't often take our most important actions—the ones necessary to get more clients and customers consistently.

Maybe you don't have a negative mindset toward sales. Perhaps you are that one person in my audience who loves the idea of being called a salesperson. Me too... now. Yet, as we'll dive into in chapter 4, worldwide data from over 2.2 million sales professionals assessed by OMG shows that the most successful salespeople have certain mindsets in common, and only 7 percent have the strong mindsets necessary to be consistently successful in any market.

Consider too that the rate of success for salespeople who meet their quotas has barely broken 50 percent, and you'll understand that there's a good chance some beliefs and mindsets about sales are hidden weaknesses in your way.

A Bad First Impression

We all have a sales story, and for most of us, it's not a good one.

My sales story started when I was growing up in a family of small business owners in Massachusetts. My mother had her own painting business restoring historic homes. My grandfather had a sporting goods store and did freelance welding work on the side—many of the universities around Boston feature his wrought iron welding. My father did freelance auto body work and created the most beautiful artwork on everything from Volkswagen vans to antique Corvettes.

But it was my father's mother, Grandma Mahoney, who was my first sales role model. In the mid-1970s, she ran one of the first women-owned real estate agencies in my home state. Growing up, my sister and I would spend part of our summer vacation with her every year. Now, if you know real estate, you know that summer is a busy time for realtors: trying to get listings, holding open houses, going to networking events, and hosting lots of private showings. Grandma Mahoney brought us along to all of it. First we'd go to the salon to get our hair done, then to the mall for new dresses, and then on to the event, where we had to abide by strict rules about what to do and say: "Don't eat too many donuts!"

By the time I was ten I knew how to introduce myself at networking events, and by twelve she had me balancing the books. Instead of playing princess dress-up, I was playing secretary with a phone and business cards.

Oh, the business cards—they were everywhere! In Grandma's purse, wallet, makeup bag, mailbox, and breadbox. She would use them for luggage tags and gift tags, and in every restaurant we went to she would leave them with the check, on bulletin boards, and on tables—even where guests were still having dinner.

And every time she saw someone she knew, she would start asking sensitive questions that made me want to disappear on the spot from embarrassment. "Oh hello, deah," Grandma would say. "You've been busy! Are you pregnant? Oh, when are you due? You know, you are going to need some moah room, and not just in the waistline... I listed this beautiful house ovah on the habah, with gorgeous views of the waddah, plenty of room to pahk all your cahs. Did hubby get the raise? What's his annual salary right now?"

I was mortified. Who asks those kinds of questions? She was always "on." And though the rest of my family would tease Grandma for her "salesy" ways, it seemed that she got what she wanted, exactly how she wanted it.

But it was the used car salesman that my mother started dating after my father passed away who sealed my perception of sales and salespeople.

My mother met Jim when I was five years old. When she moved to Maine, he came with us and got a job on a used car lot while we rented a cabin in the woods and built a house near town. He promised my mom that he would take care of my sister and me while she worked two jobs to pay the bills.

During the day, Jim would spend a few hours at the dealership, sometimes with my sister and me as we waited in the offices. All day long, I overheard sales conversations between Jim and his customers. When people came in to look at a specific car that was advertised, Jim steered them toward other cars, saying, "That one was sold this morning." Later, Jim and his boss would laugh because the ad was fake, and the car it advertised didn't exist.

When he wasn't pulling the bait-and-switch, Jim employed other common used car sales tactics with his buyers. There was the "Someone else was looking at that car this morning, it will be gone by the afternoon" strategy to create urgency. (Of course no one else had been looking at the car, but the buyer didn't know that.) Then there was the famous "Let me go talk to my manager." Oh, he did go to talk to his manager—but not about what they could do to help the buyer. They'd joke about how long they would have to wait until the buyer gave in to their price.

But I will never forget the day that a customer came in yelling and screaming that everyone at the dealership was a bunch of crooks. He had bought a car for his son and found out that the frame of the car was rotten—it was not road safe.

Jim's response? "The bill of sale says sold as-is."

Jim didn't care one bit about his customers, their safety, or how his schemes might affect them. He simply wanted the sale.

Despite all these sleazy tactics, Jim didn't make a lot of money. His reputation soon spread through the small town we lived in. When the phone rang at the house, Jim had me answer it, and if it was for him, I'd have to tell the caller that he wasn't home—because he knew it was a bill collector, or someone else he had conned.

When Jim wasn't working (if you could call it that), he spent most evenings taking us to his favorite bar, when we were barely counter height. His slimy ways were not limited to selling cars. He would pick a bar in town, run up a tab, and, when it came time to pay, he would take off and find another bar to call his favorite and run up another tab.

To Jim, taking care of us meant making sure we knew how to cook, clean, and take care of a man. In every sense of the phrase. He knew best, was never wrong, and it was always about what he wanted. And he would get what he wanted, no matter what he had to do or say.

It was these experiences that shaped the foundation of my mindset toward sales. Spending time with nosy Grandma Mahoney was exciting and uncomfortable at the same time. Spending time with pushy, slimy, sleazy used car salesman Jim was confusing and unsafe.

Whenever I heard a sales pitch, or had to deal with a salesperson, or had to engage in a sales conversation myself, this is what I thought of. I believed that, to be good in sales, you had to be pushy, slimy, and sleazy.

I wanted nothing to do with it. I avoided sales at all costs.

And that cost was high.

I wanted to get more customers or clients for my business, but I struggled to find the time, believed I needed to have the perfect messaging, and thought it was only that I hadn't yet discovered the magic process or pricing that would guarantee my success. What I didn't realize was that the thing that was really standing in my way was my mindset toward sales and what it was all about.

I learned, the hard way, that you can change your mind. When I evaluated my own mindset, I began to understand that selling isn't something we do *to* others. It is something we do *with* them.

Consider Your Sales Origin Story

To start the process of changing your sales mindset, take ten to fifteen minutes now to reflect on your own sales origin story. There is no wrong way to do this, and no right answer. In fact, your answers may come to you over time. To get started, ask yourself the questions that follow and write down whatever comes to mind first.

And yes, I want you to use pen and paper. Write it in this book if want! The physical act of writing is therapeutic, and it can help your brain form new connections and learn new processes.

If sitting still and writing is tough for you (I get it, blank pages can be intimidating!), talk these questions out with your spouse, or with neighbors, friends, or family. Or talk out loud to yourself, recording as you go. Any way you choose, ask these questions, and offer your own thoughts as they occur. Then go back and reflect on the conversation or on your train of thought, and write out your answers.

Don't skip this step! It may seem silly to you. But I promise that if you flip past this self-awareness exercise, you will find yourself trying the exercises later in this book and getting the same results you have always seen. To change what and how you think about sales, you must consider the source of your beliefs and mindsets that are leading to those thoughts and behaviors—and to your current outcomes.

Question Number 1

What do you believe sales is about? Is it about getting someone to say yes? Is it about making money? Is it about saying the right thing to make that happen? It is about having the perfect pitch or presentation that will convince them to buy?

I believe that selling is:

____

____

____

Question Number 2

What does it take to be successful in sales? Do you have to have all the right information and research? Is it product and industry knowledge? Is it having the best possible product or service? Is it having the right prices?

To succeed in sales, I need:

____

____

____

Question Number 3

What do you hate about selling? Do you dread the boring research? Or the anxiety of reaching out to people and feeling unsure about what to say? Is it the fear of being told no? Or the uncomfortable feeling of being ignored or not responded to?

I dislike these aspects of selling:

____

____

____

Question Number 4

Where does that dislike or that belief about sales come from? Was it when you had to make a major purchase and had a bad experience? (Who doesn't have at least one bad car salesperson story to tell?) Or from family dinner conversations you overheard? Or perhaps someone you knew who was in sales and was always "on"?

My beliefs and dislikes about sales come from:

____

____

____

Question Number 5

How did those experiences make you feel? Ashamed because you felt tricked? Angry because it didn't work or you felt preyed upon? Frustrated that you had to figure out how to solve your problem all over again? Confused because you don't know why people would act that way?

My experiences make me feel:

____

____

____

Once you have written down your thoughts and the source of those thoughts, step away. Take a walk or grab a glass of water—however you want to take a break. As you do, think about the fact that there are two sides to these questions: how you feel about selling, and how your potential customers feel about buying. Just like with you, there are aspects about the exchange that your customers dread.

Perhaps you have some ideas about how they feel; if so, write those down too, to refer to later. We will talk about this more in chapter 3 when you learn about the New Golden Rule and how to apply it. But, for now, I want you to plant that seed in your mind and be curious about it. You may not know the answers yet, and that's okay. Before you finish this book, you will find out. For now, let the questions sit.

KEY TAKEAWAYS AND ACTIONS

No matter our role, we are all in sales. It's normal to feel resistant to that idea when the majority of people see sales as pushy, slimy, and sleazy. To be successful in sales and change the mindsets that hinder success, we must first become aware of what our mindsets are and where those beliefs come from.

Start by reflecting on your own sales experiences and the beliefs that come with them. When you write those beliefs down, you create awareness and begin the process of rewiring your mindset.

2

NOT ABOUT YOU

The only real battle in life is
between hanging on and letting go.
SHANNON L. ALDER

"IT'S MY JOB to move metal."

Steve stared at Mr. Big, amazed at the answer the sales manager had given him. We had been searching for a used truck for weeks. After securing pre-approval for an auto loan from our credit union, we had decided on our number one choice and started the search online. But we weren't the only ones who wanted that make and model—it was hard to find. When I did find one at a dealership close to where Steve worked, I made an appointment for him stop there the next day for a test drive.

When Steve pulled into the dealership, he didn't see a single person around. There was no one outside to greet him, and he didn't see the truck anywhere. He drove around the lot, and finally found one of the model. He parked and went into the dealership and asked the first person he saw—Sean the salesman—if they were in sales—he wanted to do a test drive.

Sean took him out, and after the test drive he said to Steve, "What do we have to do today to get you into this truck?" This was in 2021! Word for word, one of the oldest lines in sales.

"Easy," my husband replied. "Come down $987. My financing is already approved and my ceiling is $35,000."

Sean invited him inside the dealership, took out his checklist, and immediately started asking about our financing rate and term.

Steve frowned. Didn't he just tell him we already had financing? Was he not listening? "Can we skip that? I have financing, you can't match it. Let's move on."

"What's your credit score?" Sean replied, looking at his checklist.

Now Steve was getting mad. This guy was not listening to him at all. "That's pretty much irrelevant, can we move the f**k on?"

Sean stood up and went to ask his manager about dropping the price by $987.

Mr. Big, the sales manager, came over. "I can't drop it $987," he stated matter-of-factly. "My job is to move metal. I bought this wholesale, and I can't budge on the price."

Steve knew, thanks to the Carfax website, that this same truck had been priced for $1,000 less the previous week. On top of that, the site had told us that this dealership was pricing the truck at $1,987 over the average market price. Steve knew that Mr. Big was lying. When Mr. Big saw that we had booked the appointment through the Carfax website, did he not realize that we would have that information?

"Well, what about my truck as a trade-in? What can you give me for that?" Steve asked.

"That truck is eleven years old," Sean replied. "It has so many miles it's almost to the moon! We could give you $1,500 for it."

The Kelley Blue Book put the trade-in value of our "to the moon" truck at $4,000. When Steve told Sean that, Mr. Big replied for him, "Sorry, can't do it."

Now Steve had a salesman on either side of him. Who should he talk to?

"You mean to tell me you can't drop $987 off a $35,000 deal?" Steve said to Mr. Big.

"The price is the price."

"The price sucks," Steve replied.

Salesman Sean referred to his checklist again. "When can you get your truck here for the trade-in?"

"Saturday at the earliest."

"Oh. Well, the truck might be gone by then!" Sean said.

"You know what?" said Steve, "Let me step outside and call my wife."

Steve was afraid that if he didn't get some fresh air he would drop another F-bomb, or worse. I could hear how mad he was as soon as he said hello, but he didn't get to say much else, because Mr. Big came outside and interrupted him. "Okay, we can do $4,000 for the trade-in on the truck, but don't forget about the fees."

I heard Steve laugh as he headed back to his car. He started to retell me what had happened so far. I suggested that maybe we should look for another model, and Steve drove around the lot and found a different vehicle that we might be interested in. He drove back to the office, went inside, and asked Sean, "Are you going to have the same sales mentality about any other truck on this lot?"

"Yes," Sean replied, not looking Steve in the eye. His manager was listening closely nearby.

No wonder sales and sellers still have such a bad reputation.

Steve's truck buying experience is yet another example of why sales continues to face distrust and negative perceptions. It's expected. And that's because the act of selling has been focused on our product or service, and what we want as sellers. Not on the buyer, and what they want.

But it doesn't have to be that way. Steve looked online and found a different truck, we contacted the dealer, and, when he showed up, the salesperson knew who Steve was, had the truck ready, and gave him what he wanted for the trade-in. Within thirty minutes, Steve was a happy truck owner. This dealership understood how to listen and ask the right questions, and how to meet their buyers where they were in their buying process.

Do your buyers feel like Steve did with the first dealer? Or, if not quite so extreme, do they feel forced into a process that doesn't align with how they buy? Are you following the checklist that you want to go through and missing what's important to them?

To find the answer to that for yourself, reach out to the prospects who stopped talking to you months ago. Send them an email or give them a call and ask, "When we talked a while back, it seemed that you were hoping to do X. Where did you end up with it?" This may spark an opportunity for you to reengage a buyer who either did nothing, or went with another solution. If they went with another solution, ask what made them choose that direction. If they did nothing, ask what was missing or stood in their way. This could be valuable information as you reengage with them or reach out to others like them.

Why It's Not about You

When I review call recordings with sellers or role-play conversations, I've found that, toward the end of the month, quarter, or year, they start to go into their product and demo pitches far too soon. When I see this happening, I ask them: "Who cares what you want?"

It's not only sellers in car lots or even in big companies who have this problem. We do it as business owners too.

Tony ran a small web design firm for lawyers. After one important sales call, he came back to me to report that, thanks to his preparations for the call, he was able to get the answers he needed to put a proposal together. He went on to list out everything that he wanted to put into the proposal, followed by what he would need to do on the next call.

As I listened, I realized that everything Tony was saying was all about him and what he wanted. I asked him, "What is their reason to make a change? How will this help them grow their business? What have they tried before? What worked, what didn't, and why?"

Tony didn't know. He thought the call had gone great because he got all the information he needed. Tony went ahead with his plan, spending days putting the proposal together and weeks more calling and emailing, trying to book the next meeting.

He never heard from them again.

Why does this happen? In a study published in 2012 in the *Proceedings of the National Academy of Sciences*, Harvard researchers Diana Tamir and Jason Mitchell discovered that we spend 40 percent of our daily interactions talking about our own thoughts, opinions, and ideas, and, when we do it, our brains are flooded with dopamine. Even when study participants were offered money to talk about something else, most of them still chose to continue talking about themselves.

What this means is that when you get your buyers to talk about themselves, you activate their brain's pleasure center, and they become more likely to trust you. Simple. But not so easy, because it means that *you* have to resist your own brain's same desire to talk about yourself.

I have to repeat this so often to my coaching clients that I created a t-shirt to help them remember that it is about the buyer, not them: it has #notaboutme printed upside down on the front so that when they wear it, they are reminded each time they look down. (Get one for yourself, your team, or that neighbor you know at bit.ly/notmetee—all proceeds are donated to a scholarship fund for women to enter sales programs at the college level.)

Selling is hard when we make it all about ourselves. It's human nature, after all. Our survival instinct is wired in our brains to look after our best interest first: "How will this impact me?"

How do you start to make it about your buyer and not about you? The first step to creating change is awareness. Take a moment now and write down the top five questions you normally ask during your sales conversations.

My top five sales questions:

1 ____

2 ____

3 ____

4 ____

5 ____

Now, take a ten-minute break. When you return, look at the questions you wrote down and ask yourself this: Do these questions get me the information I want for my own needs, or do they help me learn more about my buyer and their current circumstances? If you aren't sure of the answer, email your questions to me at e@carolemahoney.com with Buyer First Questions in your subject line for feedback.

Next, think about this: if selling isn't something you do *to* others, and is instead something you do *with* them, how could you edit these questions to focus on what your buyer cares about? For example, a common question I hear from sellers is: "When do you want this implemented by?" This helps you find out when your buyer is going to make their purchase, but it doesn't necessarily help the buyer with *their* goals. Instead, you could ask: "What type of results do you need to see, and by when?" The answer to this question can lead to more clarification questions that enable you to establish a milestone-based timeline with your buyer so they can reach their goals.

Let's say your buyer says, "I need to see results in six months." There are a number of clarification questions you can ask based on that answer, such as:

- What happens in six months if you don't see those results?
- When you do see those results in six months, what will that mean for you?
- If that happens, then what?

Let's say they respond with this: "In six months I will have to close my doors if I don't get more customers in. If that happens I will have to get a job to support my family. But if I do see those results and get that income in, then I can invest in the business to grow it more sustainably."

When most sellers hear this, they get happy ears. They are so happy to have found a problem with a big impact that they get excited to tell the buyer about their solution. But while they think they have found a way to sell them on their solution, the reality is they are missing the opportunity to document a timeline with their buyer. To make this a buyer first conversation, you have to ask additional clarification questions. Talking about the solution is creating a conversation about what *you* want to get to.

Instead of jumping to talk about all that you can do, ask questions about the steps that the buyer needs to take.

"You have six months to see results before things become dire. How long do you think it will take to get those results once you have implemented a solution like this?" When they answer, then ask: "Most of the customers we work with tell us it takes two to three months before they see results. What leads you to your conclusion?"

Your next set of clarification questions can then ask about how long to implement, how long to decide, the steps that need to happen, and the people who need to get involved.

In the following chapters, we will dig further into the specific questions you can use to reverse-engineer a timeline with your buyers. For now, take another look at the top five questions you wrote out before, and try editing them to become buyer first. How can you rephrase them to be more collaborative?

Sales Experts Are Still Figuring It Out

What you won't read in most sales books is that some of the most experienced corporate sellers and leaders struggle with the same things you struggle with.

Consider an industry that, according to authors Frank Cespedes and Yuchun Lee, spent $70 billion on training in 2017. Yet, as CSO Insights reported in 2019, only 54 percent of sellers met their goals. That average has barely moved since then.

Would you say that this industry had it figured out?

Traditional sales models and methodologies fall short because they focus on what we want and what we must do—the skills, tactics, and techniques. The supportive beliefs and mindsets you need to be successful in sales are not as commonly talked about as the other elements of sales behaviors, such as skill sets on how to prospect, qualify, and close.

Because sales methodologies and processes have been so focused on what we do, the sales profession has developed a focus on the internal workings of the company, the offering, the

Without a great buyer experience, it is extremely difficult to have a good customer experience.

value proposition, and the sales process. Companies that claim to be customer-centric still focus all their strategies on themselves, and, because of that, they hire and train their sellers the same way. It is why the dreaded product pitch is so prevalent.

The perception of sales is not getting better with technology; it's getting worse. In their recent survey of business buyers for Gartner, Brent Adamson and Nick Toman found that up to 80 percent of business customers said they prefer not to interact with a salesperson. Yet buyers still need good salespeople—in that same study, Gartner found that those buyers who preferred not to interact had a 23 percent higher rate of purchase regret.

We talk about being customer-centric. In fact, if you search LinkedIn's most popular hashtags, you will find that millions of people follow phrases such as "customer-centric" and "customer experience." But phrases about buyer experience? Less than one hundred at the time of this writing.

I aim to change that.

We seem to forget that before we can have a customer, we must have a buyer. Without a great buyer experience, it is extremely difficult to have a good customer experience. This is how companies often create the very problems they are trying to solve.

In the early days of growth at HubSpot, a sales and marketing software company based in Cambridge, Mark Roberge—author of *The Sales Acceleration Formula* and a senior lecturer at Harvard Business School—was leading sales and was concerned by the high rate of customer churn. He thought it was due to the customer experience post-sale, but his data analysis could not find any evidence of that.

When he ran the analysis against who the salesperson was, he saw that certain sellers had higher percentages of churn in their customers. That's when he realized that whether a customer stayed or left was tied to how the customer was sold and the expectations that process had set. When a mindset of "do whatever it takes to win the deal" was replaced with "do whatever it takes to do right by the buyer," retention went up.

The buying experience matters—a lot.

Yes, there are many other factors at play, but when you think about the cause as well as the symptom, mindset becomes obvious. Which makes the next thing I am about to share with you so scary.

Mindsets are contagious.

Are you familiar with the phrase "As goes the manager so goes the team"? We hear this and assume it's true, as it often matches our observation. But why does it happen?

While working with a sales manager and their team, I found that everyone on this manager's team struggled with the same weaknesses that their manager had. Curious, I analyzed a subset of Objective Management Group (OMG) performance data on over 500,000 managers and the sellers who reported to them. What I found was that when sales managers and leaders hold non-supportive beliefs (something we will dive into in future chapters), their team is 355 percent more likely to hold those same beliefs. Three hundred and fifty-five percent! These leaders could be undermining their team's performance because of their own mindsets—and not know it.

If you're thinking you can skip all this sales stuff, or that someday you'll hire sales help—employees, contractors, partners—who can handle it on your behalf, you could be creating a situation in which you will pass along your negative mindsets toward sales, and undermine the ability to sell—yours and theirs.

Big deal, though, right? When you pay a salesperson on commission, what is the risk if they don't sell anything? I suppose if you aren't counting on them to bring in revenue, there isn't any. But then why hire them?

The good news is that my analysis showed that when managers do have supportive beliefs, their teams are 1,000 percent more likely to hold those same beliefs. And those teams far outperform teams that do not have those supportive beliefs. Further analysis of deeper data showed that out of twenty-one different sales-specific competencies, top sellers have specific mindsets in common.

Data analysis from OMG of 1.1 million sellers from 11,000 companies showed that the biggest gaps between top-performing salespeople and non-performers were that they can take responsibility for their outcomes (they don't make excuses), they manage their need for approval (so they can ask the tough questions), they control their emotions (which helps them be active listeners), and they are comfortable discussing money (so that they can talk numbers with their buyers).

Success in sales isn't about who has the best prospecting tricks or the best closing techniques. It's about who has the strongest mindsets. That is what enables them to adapt to changing circumstances and buyer behaviors.

What They (Now) Teach You at Harvard Business School

The dean at Harvard Business School instituted a sales program after feedback from MBA students who were lamenting the lack of sales education they had access to after they went out into the business world. (The infamous book *What They Don't Teach You at Harvard Business School* highlighted the same issue.)

I was asked to coach Harvard MBA students in sales to help them understand that these skills are important no matter what direction they take after graduation. During the program, they were given a case study and were told they would play the buyers and sellers in a video role-play. My job as their coach was to review it and give them feedback.

As I watched the videos, I noticed that, before the role-play began, the students started off the sessions with light and easy conversation. But when it came time to start selling, they may as well have put on masks and costumes—they were different people.

> Hello Mr. Smith. Thank you for meeting with me today. I am here because we have a new best-in-market product, unlike anything before. Now I know you have limited shelf space and must have popular, high-quality products that align with your brand promise and healthy margins to reach your fiscal goals. That is why I am excited to share that these products have met all those requirements and we are prepared to offer you an exclusive partnership with margins of up to 20 percent, unheard of in your space. Would you be willing to sign this order for one hundred units today, renewable every quarter?

The students talked far too fast, pitched too soon, never took a breath to ask a question, and then immediately started discounting.

Just to be clear, this is not good sales behavior.

Don't beat yourself up if you struggle with the idea of selling, or with sales in any way. Harvard MBA students are still trying to figure it out.

There are several reasons why this happens. The first is something called the Adult Learning Model: when we are forced to learn something new, one of the ways we do it is by modeling the behaviors of those we see as successful—in this case, our idea of a successful salesperson.

When I asked the Harvard students what they thought of their videos, many replied that they thought they did well, and so did their partner. When I asked them what they would do differently, many answered that they would work on speaking more slowly.

As I started to push back on the lack of questions they asked, almost all replied with some version of "Well, isn't that what a salesperson is supposed to do? Control the call, tell them a value proposition, make the pitch, and then ask for the business?" A few thought it would be rude to ask too many questions, or felt concerned that the other person would think they didn't know what they were talking about.

Another thing that may be happening with you—and with the Harvard students—are two concepts called the Theory of Reasoned Action and the Theory of Planned Behavior. These combined psychological theories of behavior change were developed by Martin Fishbein and Icek Ajzen to explain and predict human behavior. Their research suggests that a person's behavior is determined by their intention to perform the behavior, and, more importantly, that our intentions are a function of both our attitude toward the behavior and what would be considered normal.

After coaching the Harvard students and studying these psychological theories in medical journals, I realized something. If seven out of ten of us have negative beliefs about sales, and one way we learn is by modeling the behaviors of those that we see as successful, and if the Theory of Reasoned Action and Theory of Planned Behavior say that our beliefs and what we consider normal affect how and if we will do something, then aren't we becoming and creating more of the thing we disdain?

Is this why the oldest profession in the world—sales—is also one of the most despised?

(Did that make you think of sex work? That is still sales—an exchange of value between seller and buyer...)

Is this why we avoid the things that will make us better at sales? Could it be that we spend so much time trying to find a way around it for this reason?

I couldn't tell you how many business owners and salespeople come to me for sales training and coaching and start the conversation off with: "I need to get some more clients in, but I don't want to be salesy." This is typically followed by a list of things they plan to do instead.

We try everything *but* sales. We avoid becoming better salespeople because of our beliefs about and perceptions of what sales and salespeople are. That is, we do this until we hit financial rock bottom and can't ignore it anymore, as I did in the early days of my own business.

How do you avoid doing the same? How do you pull yourself up to go at it again?

Sales got to this place because we focused solely on what we wanted, the actions we needed to take, and what a few experts claimed will work. It is time to break the cycle. At our core, pushy, slimy, and sleazy sales tactics are not who most of us are.

Selling Is Broken

The hard truth is that the sales industry is broken. And there are a lot of reasons for that.

Let's start with how sales started and evolved to where it is today. Consider that, and you will see why I didn't include anything in this book that is not backed by research and that I haven't tested in the field myself.

At the very first World Salesmanship Congress, which took place in Detroit in 1916, the goal was to examine the sales methodologies for "business betterment through betterment in salesmanship." (Clearly, no marketers were involved in that mission statement.) One of the methodologies explored was the "Science of Selling," a concept introduced by Grant Nablo. He proposed the application of phrenology—the study of the shape and size of the cranium as a supposed indication of character and mental abilities. This method became so popular that the Ford Motor Company adopted it, producing a primer for

The hard truth is that **the sales industry is broken.**

its sales force in 1923 that was called *Ford Products and Their Sale*. The manual contained the following instruction: "Sell the vehicle according to the shape of the prospect's head. High foreheads leave room for larger development and indicate people who are less likely to resist new ideas."

This is the science of selling? You can't make this stuff up!

When the Great Depression hit in the late 1920s, many turned to a career in sales because it was an easy job to get. There wasn't much in the way of formal sales training, so people were left to figure it out on their own. This is where methodologies such as Mood Selling became popular—especially among Bible and encyclopedia salesmen. I call it the guilt sale. A salesman might show up at your door and explain how buying a Bible would save your soul because it would help the salesman feed his starving kids—whom he often brought with him. You felt sympathy, so you bought a Bible.

To be fair, it wasn't all bad. It was in the 1920s that Albert E. Teetsel worked with the Fuller Brush Company and brought the concept of positive thought to his sales teams. Each distributor had to sign a pledge that said, among other things, that the salesperson's obligation "is one of service to the customer, to the company I represent, and to the community in which I live and work," and that "I will be courteous; I will be kind; I will be sincere; I will be helpful." The commercial and popular success of the company was built on this focus on its people, in particular the sales team. The Fuller Brush Man has a special place in my heart.

With the 1930s came the famous Dale Carnegie book, *How to Win Friends and Influence People*. Thanks to that, we have the foundation of Customer-Centric Selling.

Unfortunately, this is when the practice of paying salespeople on commission came into play. Some believe that this is what changed the paradigm, because this was the same time that the "barrier method" of selling became popular.

I particularly dislike this methodology due to its manipulative nature—it creates a "barrier" to the ability of buyers to say no. Sellers will ask customers leading questions for which the only logical answer is yes. Once they get a series of "yes" responses, they then throw in the key question: "And, of course, you want to do this right away, don't you?"

This manipulates buyers in two ways. First, the seller will often arrange to make sure that the spouse or child of the buyer is present—a tactic that insurance salespeople have become notorious for using. You have heard the questions before. "Obviously, if something happened to you, you would want your partner to be looked after. Wouldn't you?" Who would say no to that? Especially with their partner present! Encyclopedia Britannica salespeople did it too. They would never attempt to sell a set without the children there, so they could "trap" the buyer with questions like: "Obviously, you want your child to have the very best education possible, don't you?"

This worked because, at the time, salespeople still largely controlled the information that buyers had. There were no laws protecting buyers, hence *caveat emptor*—"let the buyer beware." Salespeople made claims and promises and used whatever techniques and methods they could to get a deal, typically with few to no consequences because a large portion of a salesperson's income at the time (often as much as 90 percent) was based on their ability to close the deal. And so salespeople were willing to risk everything, with little thought to the buyer's remorse that customers might suffer as a result of their activities.

Eventually, governments stepped in and established the buyer's right to a cooling-off period, making it easier to get out of the agreements they were manipulated into.

Alphabet Soup

It does get a little better. I mean, if sales methodology started with the size of someone's forehead, it couldn't get worse—could it?

As the decades went on, popular sales methodologies tried to adapt to economic circumstances and the reactions of buyers. With the decline of Barrier Selling, the years between the 1930s and the 1990s became packed with an alphabet soup of acronym-filled sales methodologies that all claimed to improve performance. But the damage was done: the early teachings had created a foundation where sales were seemingly easier for the seller, at the expense of the buyer.

In the 1950s it was ADAPT—Assessment, Discovery, Activation, Projection, Transition. Then it was David Ogilvy's AIDA Selling, an approach to get Attention, Interest, Desire, and Action. Following that, in the 1960s, there was Need Satisfaction Selling from Don Hammalian and the Xerox Corporation, which was a seven-step process to uncover needs and introduce benefits.

In the 1970s, Strategic Selling was developed by the Miller Heiman Group; this method used a fixed planning process to highlight danger areas and penetrate the decision-making process. Consultative Selling—or SPIN (Situation, Problem, Impact, Need)—from Neil Rackham came about in the 1990s and is still popular today. It is based on in-depth questioning techniques to understand customer pain, and then consulting to help the buyer see the impact for themselves.

From 1990 to now, most popular methodologies have been versions of the previous ones: Solution Selling, the Challenger Sale, BANT, MEDDIC, SNAP, Value Selling, Sandler Selling, Relationship Selling, Referral Selling—the list is seemingly never-ending. And if you do a Google search for best sales methodologies, you will see results filled with "The Top 10..." or "12 Best..." or "Tried and True..." Each has different steps, different opinions, and differing results. How would you be able to choose which is right for your buyer and your business?

The easy answer: none. Overall, buyers aren't impressed with any of them.

In their 2021 *State of Sales Report*, LinkedIn notes that 65 percent of sellers they surveyed said they "always" put the buyer first.

But only 23 percent of buyers surveyed agreed.

Buyers in the LinkedIn survey shared some of the behaviors that turned them off from making a purchase, including 48 percent who named misleading information about a product and/or its price and 44 percent who felt the seller didn't understand their company and what they needed.

In a separate 2020 report, LinkedIn noted that the number one trait that buyers value in sellers is active listening. But when managers ranked the importance of traits in sellers they hire, they listed active listening last.

Last! Clearly there is a wide chasm between the way we sell and the way we prefer to buy.

That's the crazy thing about this, isn't it? We are all both buyers and sellers, yet when we are in one role, we forget what it's like to be in the other. Why does this happen?

Consider the history of sales training. Until now, sales methods and tactics have been based on the observations of a few.

You could compare the state of sales today to how doctors were trained and perceived before the Renaissance. Frankly, they were seen as barbarians or religious fanatics. Few trusted them, but, when people were sick and desperate, they saw doctors as a necessary evil; there were no other choices. It wasn't until the medical profession started applying scientific theory and teaching medicine through experimentation and practice that doctors started to get the level of respect and trust they take for granted today.

Likewise, the findings in this book are based on sales-specific data and research in the behavioral sciences that my clients and I have tested in real life. I'm not saying this is an exact science, like geometry or chemistry. But by basing our strategies in science and continuing to test them, we have a better chance of knowing what worked, why, and how to make it better going forward.

There is one bit of alphabet soup that is still alive and well in the sales profession today, actively feeding the masculine culture, and it needs to finish its dying breath. Most of the time, when people hear I am in sales, their next words quote the infamous movie *Glengarry Glen Ross*: "Oh yeah, Always Be Closing—love that movie!" which is then typically followed by a slap on the back.

Well, enough of that old ABC. Today, the new mantra is Always Be Collaborating. When you collaborate with your buyers, you change your world and theirs—for the better. That means—as I have said—shifting your mindset toward sales from something you do *to* buyers to something you do *with* them.

Breaking this cycle and the perception of sales as pushy, slimy, and sleazy will require this specific mindset shift if you want to get to the behavioral change you need to make to reach your goals. Every chapter in this book will give you strategies and tactics to change those mindsets, adopt new behaviors, and get better outcomes by collaborating with your prospective buyers.

But changing your sales behavior is like changing other behaviors—the kinds of things you make New Year's resolutions about, such as weight loss. How do you make it stick in the long term?

Break the Cycle

Throughout my childhood and most of my adult life, I struggled with my weight.

That's a nice way to say what my doctors said: Obese. Prediabetic. High risk for stroke and heart attack.

I could point to a lot of reasons for this: genetics, previous sports injuries, sitting at a desk most of the day. I tried every diet you could think of. WeightWatchers, Zone, South Beach, Keto, Paleo, Whole30, and that weird shake that tastes like cake batter. With each one, after some initial weight loss, it would all come back. Sometimes I would gain even more.

At age forty-five, I decided to try again. I had heard the ads for Noom that promised no fad diets and weight loss that would stay off—using psychology. In case you haven't guessed, I love psychology. I was in.

When I started the program, they offered daily education articles based on research. I was surprised to find that it was the same research I use to help business owners, sellers, and leaders get better at sales. If it can work for my clients to help them change their behavior, maybe I could apply it to losing the weight and keeping it off?

It started with my goals. Instead of what size or weight I wanted to be, I focused on how I wanted to feel. I knew that the scale would go up and down. In the past, I had focused on losing a pound a week (get 1 percent better every day!), then I'd give up when the scale would go down one week only to creep back up the next. When I instead focused on how I felt after I ate something good for me, or after I took a walk, that immediate positive feedback kept me going toward my goal. (We'll dive deeper into this in chapters 8 and 9.)

The program included education about the psychology of weight loss, which is the psychology of most behavior change.

It's not about a hack, a trick, or a fad—we know what we need to do to lose weight, but our mindsets either help or hinder us from doing what we know we should. It was more about getting control of my health and feeling better, not about how I looked or what others thought of me. And there was daily exercises and homework to do, combined with tracking my food (behaviors) and weight (outcomes). I still do these daily tracking activities today.

As Katy Milkman, a Wharton psychology professor and the author of *How to Change*, writes, "Achieving transformational behavioral change is more like treating chronic illness than curing a rash."

How I lost the weight is a similar process to how my clients change their sales mindsets, behaviors, and results—and how I did too. And now you can do the same.

This isn't about going on a "sales diet" or using the latest fad; it's about changing your sales lifestyle and daily behaviors. The first step is to become aware of what your current habits and routines are, and how they impact you.

Here's a first exercise to look at your habits and mindset. I first heard about the "we-we" factor from Jeffrey and Bryan Eisenberg, authors of *Waiting for Your Cat to Bark?* Now, when my coaching clients ask me what I think of their email, pitch, or cold-call script, I ask them to calculate their "we-we" factor.

Here's how it works. If you are actively making sales calls now, record one and audit how much time you spend talking versus the other person. Are you doing most of the talking? Is there a back-and-forth exchange between the two of you?

Next, scan for how often you use the words "me," "we," "our," and "I." These are "me-focused" words. Write that number here: ____________

Now assess how often you use the words "you," "yours," "because," and "that means." These are "buyer-focused" words. Write that number here: ___________

Are your "me-focused" words greater than your "buyer-focused" words? If so, that may mean you are we-we-ing all over yourself, and that turns buyers off. Edit your language to include more "buyer-focused" words and observe how your interactions change. You may find that people become more open to sharing, that they respond more, and that they are willing to talk with you longer.

This simple shift in language can break the cycle of slimy and start a buyer first mindset.

KEY TAKEAWAYS AND ACTIONS

We are hard-wired to think of ourselves first. This, combined with the history of sales methodology, has created today's negative perception of sales. Unfortunately, it continues, because in our desire for success, we follow the teachings of a few we see as successful—even if it means we have to be pushy, slimy, and sleazy. When we shift our mindsets to put buyers first, we build trust and value with them.

To begin the mindset shift that sales is not something we do *to* others and is instead something we do *with* them, audit your questions and calls to become aware of how much you talk about yourself versus how much your buyers talk about themselves.

As you work through the key actions in this book, share your insights, questions, and wins with me on social media using the hashtags #buyerfirst and #notaboutme.

3

FOLLOW THE NEW GOLDEN RULE

Whoever has the gold makes the rules.

THE WIZARD OF ID

WHEN I WAS diagnosed with hypothyroidism and then thyroid cancer, I had my thyroid surgically removed. The next ten years were spent bouncing from one doctor to the next, with no clear answers on how to get my metabolism, memory, and energy back. A typical doctor's visit would mean weeks to get my medical records from one doctor to the next, and, despite that, I would still have to show up and spend twenty minutes describing my medical history, followed by another ten-minute wait in the lobby for them to call me into an exam room. Why did I go through all of the work to have records sent in advance if they weren't going to look at them?

After one fifteen-minute wait in a paper gown in an exam room, the doctor came in with their head bent over a folder containing my test results. Finally, some answers! But no, the doctor told me that my blood work all came back normal—my symptoms must be due to something else.

Then, another ten minutes going through their checklist of symptoms: Yes, I am tired all the time. No, I can't focus. Yes, I forget things. No, I can't lose weight. What about a different brand of hormone supplements—the last doctor mentioned that could be the issue?

"I don't know why your other doctor said that. Everything looks normal in your blood work. Your symptoms are due to your obesity. Have you considered a weight-loss program?"

A forty-five-minute wait for fifteen minutes with a doctor who didn't listen to me and told me the same thing everyone else did. When did doctors start to act as if they were used car salespeople?

Isn't this how you feel when you engage with sellers who don't do any research on you, who ask questions but don't have any answers that are different from what you've heard and tried, or who diagnose your problem without understanding anything outside of what their checklist says?

I decided to forgo traditional medicine and went to a holistic doctor. When I arrived, the receptionist knew my name and said they would be right with me. Five minutes later I was sitting with the doctor, fully clothed, as he reviewed my medical records with me. He asked about how I felt, what I thought the cause was, and what I had tried before. He asked about my day-to-day to get a sense of what was doable for me. "You know your body better than anyone else. What do you feel is happening?"

I was speechless (for once in my life). No doctor had ever asked me that before.

"Everyone keeps telling me that my thyroid hormone levels are normal, but I don't feel normal. Something is missing—as if it's taking too long for the medication to kick in, and, when it does, it's all at once and usually when I am trying to go to bed."

He recommended some new tests and explained what he hoped to learn from them.

When I came back for the follow-up visit, he explained how my body reacts differently to certain medications and that I was lacking the ability to absorb my hormone replacement supplement. "It's like a carburetor in a motor engine that is getting plenty of fuel, but not enough air to spark so it floods out. We can discuss diet changes and exercise routines, but what do you feel you can change that is doable for you right now?" Together we came up with plan that involved a new hormone, some additional supplements, and a few dietary changes.

A week later I started to feel better, had some energy, and got my focus back. This was the start of a health journey that led me to lose 105 pounds over the next two years. At my last checkup he remarked that he hadn't seen such near-perfect blood results.

All because he listened and collaborated with me to come up with a plan that worked for me, and because I was willing and open to change.

You can do the same with your buyers when you shift to a buyer first mindset and collaborate with them.

But change is hard. Especially big, long-term change. That's why quick wins that show you are going in the right direction are key (for you and your buyers!).

I'm going to show you four key areas where my coaching clients have found quick wins to help them shift their mindsets and engage with buyers in ways that those buyers found valuable.

These quick wins are your opportunity to build your confidence. With each small step of progress, your belief in your ability to make the mindset and behavioral changes grows. The work you do in the pages ahead will get tough, and at times you may doubt yourself. In those moments, look for the bright spots. It may be that you did something new, or someone's response to you changed. Make note of these small changes to help you build up to bigger ones.

Collaboration Builds Trust

Trust is a funny thing, isn't it? Fleeting. That's because it is a feeling, and feelings happen because of the chemicals in our brains.

When we open ourselves up to trust, it makes us feel warm, welcome, and safe—all due to the explosions of feel-good dopamine chemicals in the caudate nucleus, the pleasure center of our brains. This is the place in our brains where relationship attachments happen.

And in the reverse, when we are afraid and do not trust, we feel disconnected, hesitant, and alone. The chemicals that cause us to feel this live in our "reptilian brain," a place called the amygdala. We freeze up, can't think, and certainly can't take action to move forward. It's fight-or-flight time.

In his book *The Code of Trust*, FBI behavioral analyst Robin Dreeke says that all of our relationships and encounters are affected by our biology of beliefs and emotions. We describe it as chemistry, and that is exactly what trust is: chemistry. How we act creates the trust chemicals in others.

This chemistry can work for you or against you, depending on how you make people feel trust. The verbal and non-verbal messages you send to inspire trust enforce both the power of your message and the trustworthiness of the messenger. You.

When I visited my new doctor, I didn't feel pressured or frustrated; instead, I felt listened to and valued. When was the last time you felt you were being sold to? How did the seller act? Did they do most of the talking? If you recall the Harvard study from chapter 2, we spend a lot of time talking about ourselves because, when we do, our brains reward us with dopamine. But it works both ways: when you get others to talk about *their* opinions, experiences, and ideas, you make them feel good.

When you take the focus away from yourself, you naturally become more collaborative with your buyers. Instead of telling them what they should do, know, or think, you start asking them more questions about what they think they should do. That makes it easier for them to trust you, and they need to be able to trust you if they are going to buy from you. If they trust you, they will be open to hearing what your expert advice is, and eager to let you help guide them.

Collaboration with others requires putting their interests before your own. The focus must first be on them, and not you or what you want—or on your products and services. This is the foundational mindset shift you will need to make to get more, and better, clients and customers. Selling is an exchange of value. And since your buyers are the ones with the money, it is their determination of value that counts. They have the gold, so they make the rules. This is the New Golden Rule.

Your role as a seller is to help people buy solutions to solve their problems. That means you are helping them manage change. Remember the Gartner survey from earlier? Among the 1,000 B2B buyers surveyed, 80 percent "voiced uncertainty in their own ability to manage such change." You must help your buyers make decisions. There is a process to how people make buying decisions, and if you follow the New Golden Rule, that means you must change how you sell—in mindset, process, and techniques.

In their book *Stop Selling & Start Leading*, authors James Kouzes, Barry Posner, and Deb Calvert surveyed 530 business buyers to find out what behaviors buyers wanted from sellers. They found that buyers strongly preferred seller behaviors that invited collaboration, enabled the co-creation of new ideas, and fostered new ways of looking at problems.

For these reasons, the buyer first mindset has an impact on nearly every aspect of your business.

Quick Win: Ask More Questions Than You Think You Need

Active listening and asking sequential questions are two of the most common behavioral changes I see with clients who embrace the buyer first mindset and unlock unlimited results. One way I teach them to do this is with the Questions and Periods Game.

The rules are simple: When someone asks you a question, you answer that question with another question. But it must be relevant to the first question asked—a clarification of their own question.

When I first started doing this in my business, I didn't have a lot of buyers to have conversations with or to practice my question asking. I decided to practice on everyone around me, which was usually my husband.

Typically, Steve would come home, greet the dog, grab a couple of beers, and trek down the stairs to my home office. If I wasn't on the phone, he would announce that it was "break time." He'd tell me about his day, and issues he had at work. As a management consultant and coach, I couldn't resist offering him advice. "You should talk to your boss about that and say this..." Annoyed, he'd tell me I had no idea how it worked at his workplace or what a given person was like—"That would never work."

As I was beginning the work on my own sales mindsets and behaviors, he came home one day and, instead of telling him what to do, I asked him questions: "Have you tried this?" or "What if you said that, how do you think they would react?"

"I hadn't thought of that," he'd say. "I'll try it out."

I started practicing asking questions on hubby after work every day. For the first few days, he didn't notice. The day he did, he began to turn it right around on me: If I'd ask, "Hey, can you do this for me?" he would reply, mockingly: "Do you *want* me to do that for you?" Dammit! He saw me. I had to get better at asking my questions. It was a matter of paying attention to details, tone of voice, and timing.

Eventually, we turned it into a New Year's Eve drinking game. If you answered a question with a period, you had to take a shot.

It was a very quick game!

It didn't take long for the kids to pick up on the game too. (No shots for them; they were ten and twelve at the time.) Soon, our dinner conversations became entertaining and educational.

Practice asking questions of the people around you. Resist the urge to talk about yourself until they ask. Don't be surprised when more people want to be your friend.

Freedom from Rejection

Taking the focus off ourselves and putting the buyer first can change what we dislike about selling, because realizing it is not about us takes the pressure off. It curbs the need for approval from others, or to been seen as smart or likeable. It doesn't matter what others think about us, because it's not about us. It's about our buyer and their problem. *Their* problem—not ours.

Think about the times you felt nervous. What did you think about? What they thought of you? How you looked? How you sounded? Do you remember the weight of it?

Now think about a time when you felt silly. Did you care what others thought? Or did you let go and do whatever you felt, or whatever you had to do to make someone else laugh? Did you feel lighter, freer, without a care?

That is the difference between being us-focused and other-focused. Because being other-focused doesn't only benefit them. It helps us as well.

The "daily rejection" is something most people dislike about sales. When you are other-focused and rejection happens—and you know it will—that rejection isn't a judgment of our value or worth, it's simply not the right time or solution for them right now. It's not about us!

Quick Win: Go for No

This phrase "Go for No" comes from my colleague Andrea Waltz, coauthor of a book with the same title. We naturally look for the reason why a buyer should or would say yes to us. We ask carefully phrased questions that lead them to our solution, or we only hear the things that we know we can do, and don't take the rest into account. We don't want to know about the "no." But we should.

One exercise I have clients go through is creating their "dirty laundry list." This is a list of all the reasons why a buyer doesn't make a decision (or struggles to), why a buyer wasn't successful with their solution—whether a competitor's solution or their own—and all the reasons why the seller lost an opportunity to a competitor, or to the status quo (meaning the buyer does nothing). Whatever reason that something went wrong, it goes on the dirty laundry list. These are all the possible "no"s you could get.

With that list in hand, the next task is to form questions that address or dig into any of those issues, concerns, or challenges. (Often this list is where your best content and other resources will come from for your sales messaging and marketing efforts.)

This is what I mean by "go for no": bring up the "no"s before your buyer does. If your buyer brings them up first, your chances of working with them could go down significantly.

One of my clients, let's call him Eric, often lost customers because they didn't have the time or staff to run his software. After a few coaching sessions on how to use this as a question in his process, he brought it up in his next sales conversation.

"Some clients have struggled with this solution because they didn't have the time to do everything. How will you allocate the time, or find help to implement your strategy?"

Surprised, the buyer answered that they hadn't considered that and asked for Eric's recommendation. Eric had immediately built trust with the buyer, because he showed them that he didn't want to sell a solution they wouldn't be successful with. He was willing to face the rejection, because it wasn't about him or his solution—it was about their ability to reach their goals.

Do this for yourself now and write down your answers to the questions that follow.

The last time you lost a deal or a client wasn't happy, what was the reason?

____

____

How will you phrase that reason as a question in your next sales conversation?

____

____

Communication Clarity

When you are truly buyer first, your marketing and sales messaging and where to put the message becomes clear. It is a beacon as you try to navigate how and where to spend your focus, time, and money.

Trying to write this book over the past decade, I have started, stopped, and started again a half dozen times. I would write out what I believed the outline should be, what I wanted to tell people, and kept hitting a wall. *What if people don't think it's good? What if people criticize it as a waste of paper? Or worse, what if no one notices?* Then I heard Anjanette "AJ" Harper, author of *Write a Must-Read* and developmental editor and publishing strategist at the Top Three Book Workshop, say the words I tell all my clients: "It's not about you."

I talk about a buyer first mentality. AJ Harper talks about a "reader first" mentality. She says that a book that transforms people isn't about something; it is for someone. Every chapter and every teaching point is to serve them, not to make you look good.

I needed to follow my own advice.

Once I applied that to how I looked at this book, what to write became clear. I decided on what to include or not include based on how it helped you, my reader. The voices that had been whispering doubts got a slap in the face when I reminded them who this was for and what they were struggling with.

Pause for a moment here and think of the one person you know that your solution would help. What do they struggle with? How do they see things? If you are not sure, reach out to them and ask them. More on this in chapter 5.

Quick Win: Focus on the Person, Not the Demographic

Have you ever been speaking with someone at a networking meeting and asked, "Who is your best customer?" What type of response did you get? Was it "Anyone who..." or "CEOs of midsized companies..."?

Doesn't that answer make it difficult to recognize or identify who to look for?

Are you the person who answers that way?

Next time someone asks you this, there is a better framework to use. Fill in the blanks that follow to use it yourself.

"I work best with <title/role> ____________

who are <emotional descriptor> ____________

with <problem> ____________

and are <personality descriptor> ____________.

Who is the first person that comes to mind for you, <First Name>?"

You might be wondering how to fill in those descriptors. Think about who you have loved to work or talk with that is in the role your ideal buyer has now. What attitude did they have? How did they approach things?

Write down that person's name and why they came to mind. If it helps, put a sticky note right here in the book as a reminder to reach out to them later.

I enjoyed working and talking with:

____

They came to mind because:

____

____

____

Focus on that single person as your ideal customer, not on some broad demographic—that will make it easier for people you network with to think of someone who fits that description. If they don't know anyone, ask who they know that might know someone similar.

For example, when I get asked who my best customer is, I might reply, "I love working with business owners who are passionate about their work but overwhelmed and frustrated with their efforts to get customers and clients. They are smart, curious, and open-minded about using data and research to understand the root cause of their struggle. Who is the first person you know that comes to mind?"

Consistency and Predictability

Revolving how you sell around your buyer not only builds trust, frees you from rejection, and makes your messaging more clear, it also helps make your strategy and results more predictable and consistent.

Traditional sales methodologies and processes are inside out: they start with what the company or seller wants and how they want to sell, just as Sean the car salesman did with his checklist. He ignored Steve's process, questions, and responses and instead went to the next question on his list.

When we ignore our buyer's process and where they are in it, our follow-up doesn't add value to the buyer's experience. Instead, we come across as a pest or a nag—like a kid in a store who begs their parents to give them something they want and will not let up. Somehow, we believe that the more persistent—the pushier—we are, the more we follow up, check in, look for an update, the more we try to pull them toward us to say yes, the more likely that they will. The reality is that, when we're pushy, we push people away, and it slows the whole sales process down.

In his book *The Science of Selling*, David Hoffeld reviewed 400 studies and found that, when making decisions, buyers feel confident and comfortable when they can answer the following questions for themselves:

1. **Why do I need to make a change?** What is the problem we are trying to fix, or opportunity we are trying to gain?
2. **Why do I need to do it now versus later?** What will happen if I don't do it now? Is that so bad? If the current situation continues, when will it become too big of a problem to easily fix?
3. **Why should I spend the money?** Why not do it myself? Can I do it? Is there any downside? Is it worth it to have someone else do it?

When we're pushy, we push people away, and it slows the whole sales process down.

4. **Why is this solution the best option?** What is the best way to fix it, or achieve it?
5. **Why this product or service?** What other options do I have? Why these options?

Later, in chapters 6 and 7, we will dive deeper into these questions and more so you that you can ask them to your buyers inside the natural flow of a conversation.

As Mark Roberge—that senior lecturer at Harvard Business School—has said to his students: "We need to turn our sales process from the inside-out to the outside-in and align how we sell with how today's buyer makes decisions."

Quick Win: Reverse-Engineer Your Buyer's Process

The most common complaint I get from salespeople and business owners is when buyers stop responding to them. My first question in response is, "When did they need to see results by?"

Often, I'll get replies about when they want the solution implemented or when they want to make the decision by. Not about results at all. A simple question, but one that few have answers to after their sales calls.

Make this one of your earliest questions in your next sales conversation. Without that answer, you will likely be chasing them down for updates, and leaving desperate emails and voicemails for them to get back to you. Why? Because you don't have a destination and date that you are working toward together.

Let's say you ask this question, and they tell you they need to see results in six months. Great! Now, what is the next question that comes to mind?

What happens in six months?

Why is this important? It is the compelling reason to change, the urgency to make something happen. With that reason and date, you can now reverse-engineer their buying process with them by asking questions like these:

- How long after the solution is implemented would you expect to see results by? How will you measure progress toward those results to know if you are on track?
- What happens in that time if you don't see those results? Or, when you do see those results, what will that mean for you?
- Given your current resources (time, budget, people), how long do you feel the implementation should take? Who needs to get involved and when from your side?
- To see X results by <date> and with an implementation schedule of Y, how confident are you that you and your team will be able to make your decision by <date>?
- What might be an obstacle? How will we work through it?
- What other options are you considering? What criteria will you use to decide? Who is typically involved in these types of decisions?
- What is most important to them to feel confident in their choice?

No amount of following up or nagging is compelling—if you have kids, then you know what I mean. But by sharing these specific details with you, they have created what psychologists call a commitment device. When we don't do the things that we say we will, it makes us uncomfortable. You will learn more about this in later chapters.

KEY ACTIONS AND TAKEAWAYS

Value is in the eye of the buyer. They make the rules now—and that is a good thing. When you know their rules, sales success is less mysterious and more predictable. You don't have to know it all, but you have to know enough to be able to collaborate with your buyers—which is where they place the most value.

To build your confidence in your ability to shift your sales mindsets and see different results, look for your own quick wins in asking more and better questions that include reasons why they might say no and focusing on your best buyers—rather than on *any* buyer.

GET YOUR HEAD IN THE GAME

Our greatest battles are that with our own minds.
JAMESON FRANK

STEPHANIE WAS SITTING next to me on a two-hour train ride from New York City to Poughkeepsie, and asked what was bringing me upstate.

"A writing retreat!" I said, pointing to this manuscript on my screen.

She politely asked more about the retreat, what the book was about, and what I did for work.

"It's for business owners who are frustrated because they've tried everything to get new clients and customers and don't realize that it's their mindsets toward sales that are getting in their way."

Stephanie raised her eyebrows, a smile in her eyes over her face mask. "Do you know what I do? I lead sales at Tiffany's." (Yes, the luxury store.) "And I might argue that it's more than business owners who struggle—I have seen it happen in my sales team as well."

She went on to tell me about one of her sellers who was struggling, though she had the same abilities and resources as her peers. This salesperson would often say, "I don't know what I'm doing wrong. I'm just not a good salesperson, and this department has always struggled."

Do you feel the same way as Stephanie's seller? Have you repeated those same thoughts to yourself? Maybe you don't know what to do. It could be that you are not a good salesperson...

Yet.

Stephanie told me how she challenged her seller's thinking and encouraged her to change her mindsets and thought patterns to believe that she could change things and make improvements.

Within a few months, Stephanie noticed some changes. The salesperson was holding herself differently, was talking slower and less, was more calm, and was asking more and better questions of her coworkers and in her sales conversations with buyers. Before long, she became the top seller on the team and rose in the company to become a leader herself.

Simply by changing her mindsets. And so can you, with that one little word.

Yet.

The Placebo Effect on Sales Success

Stress has a huge impact on our physical and mental health. Some studies suggest that stress can weaken our immune system, cause inflammation, and—for some—lead to a recurrence of cancer. I know for myself that my own thyroid cancer was diagnosed a year after I started my business—the most stressful year of my life. What we think and feel impacts us physically.

For further proof, consider the placebo effect. The placebo effect isn't only about positive thinking, or simply believing a treatment or procedure will work. As Ted Kaptchuk, a professor at the Beth Israel Deaconess Medical Center, says in an article published by Harvard Medical School, the placebo effect is "about creating a stronger connection between the brain and body and how they work together."

"When you look at these studies that compare drugs with placebos, there is the entire environmental and ritual factor at work," says Kaptchuk. "You have to go to a clinic at certain times and be examined by medical professionals in white coats. You receive all kinds of exotic pills and undergo strange procedures. All this can have a profound impact on how the body perceives symptoms because you feel you are getting attention and care."

You can give yourself a placebo too. Kaptchuk has found that practicing self-care is helpful: "Engaging in the ritual of healthy living—eating right, exercising, yoga, quality social time, meditating—provides some of the key ingredients of a placebo effect."

When you combine how and what you think with self-care routines, you can change your mindset and your reality.

Change your mind, change your life.

Now, you might be thinking, as I did once upon a time, that you are self-aware and would never let your beliefs about sales get in your way. Maybe you don't avoid sales because you have a negative perception, as I did. Perhaps you see it as a necessary evil, or you have a plan to do it differently with your business model and offering. It might be that you don't disdain sales at all, but you've hit some walls and roadblocks. You don't have to hate the idea of sales to have beliefs and mindsets that get in your way of collaborating with your buyer so that you can both reach your goals.

What you may not realize is that some of your common, everyday thought patterns are counterproductive to being an effective seller.

But which thoughts and activities are the ones you need to change?

In my work with business owners, sellers, and sales leaders over the past two decades, I have used sales-specific data from Objective Management Group (OMG), which at the time of this writing has evaluated over 2.2 million sales professionals on twenty-one sales competencies in both mindset and skill set with 282 attributes contributing to those competencies. Over the past thirty years, they have identified the "Sales DNA" mindsets that multiple third-party audits prove can predict sales performance. These DNA elements, or fundamental sales mindsets, exist on a spectrum. Some are a big obstacle, and others slightly less. The one thing that all these Sales DNA mindsets have in common is that they are rooted in beliefs. Non-supportive beliefs are the most common weakness among sales professionals. Belief is the placebo effect on your sales performance. Unfortunately, you, me, and 85 percent of professional sellers worldwide don't have them. Instead, we have non-supportive beliefs that, instead of helping us, hinder the development of specific mindsets toward sales and the behaviors necessary to see results with buyers. If left unchallenged and unchanged, these non-supportive beliefs will prevent you from doing the things you know you should and can do in the moments that matter the most.

In the following pages, I will give you examples of a few of these non-supportive beliefs, explain how they impact your mindsets and sales behaviors, and show you how this can cause the buyer behaviors you might be seeing. When you see these buyer behaviors, pay attention to the sales thoughts or beliefs that sound familiar to you; these are the ones you will need to

Change
your mind,
change
your life.

actively counter and replace with new beliefs. To know if this is something that hinders your sales success, look at the possible impact that has. Make note of where in your conversations it happens. That will become the thing you will need to practice—which we will talk about more in chapter 6.

Now, what about the fundamental mindsets that those beliefs impact?

Mindset Number 1: Emotional Involvement

It is natural to first think how something impacts us; unfortunately, that belief limits your ability to control your emotions. When you are emotionally involved in a sale, it takes you out of the present. You think about the future, or the next step. You are not in the present moment and hearing what your prospect is saying, including the tone and inflection of their voice. You are losing your objectivity and your ability to offer insight, and instead developing happy ears that tell you what you want to hear. ("They're ready to buy!") This inhibits your ability to actively listen and ask questions with ease. You will likely get frustrated and try to "move things along," only to push away prospects with your tactics. As a result, you may notice that people ignore you and don't respond to your emails and voicemails.

The Results of Your Current Belief

Belief	Mindset	Behavior	Result
"How does this impact me?"	Emotional involvement	Loss of objectivity and ability to listen	Buyers ignore you; don't respond

The Results of a New Belief

Belief	Mindset	Behavior	Result
"It's not about me."	Emotional management	Active listening	Buyers feel understood and become willing to engage

Mindset Number 2: Approval Seeking

Do you believe that people need to like you to buy from you? If so, you are setting yourself up for failure. Your fear of being disliked inhibits all of the necessary sales skills that allow you to engage in meaningful conversations. Because you have a need for approval—or a need for people to see you a certain way—you may find yourself saying what you think they want to hear. You won't ask tough questions, which means you can't be authentic or viewed as trustworthy. As a result, you may find it difficult to get buyers to share information with you.

The Results of Your Current Belief

Belief	Mindset	Behavior	Result
"People need to like me."	Approval seeking	Telling them what they want to hear	Buyers lose trust; will not share information

The Results of a New Belief

Belief	Mindset	Behavior	Result
"My worth is not based on approval."	No need for approval	Able to ask tough questions	Buyers seek your advice

Mindset Number 3: Non-Supportive Buy Cycle

Then there is a non-supportive buy cycle, or, as I call it, the "how you buy is how you sell" mindset. Are you the type of person who must have the best price, compare features, or delay decisions to think a purchase over? If so, then you can certainly understand when a prospect wants to do the same thing, right? How you behave as a buyer will impact your ability to sell—and, if you are a leader, the way you buy will influence how your team sells. For example, you may find yourself dealing with buyers who delay decisions and seem to keep coming up with reasons why they can't decide now, and your own similar behaviors prevent you from questioning them further.

The Results of Your Current Belief

Belief	Mindset	Behavior	Result
"I have to have the best price."	Non-supportive buy cycle	Accept stalls and put-offs	Buyers delay decisions

The Results of a New Belief

Belief	Mindset	Behavior	Result
"Value isn't about price."	Supportive buy cycle	Push back on stalls and excuses	Buyers make decisions faster

Mindset Number 4: Discomfort Discussing Money

Many of us were raised to believe that it is rude to talk about money. This belief becomes a mindset issue when you need to discuss return on investment (ROI) with your buyers, or when your buyer says that you are too expensive. Instead of helping a prospect focus on the value of solving the problem, you avoid it and say, "I'll email you the proposal." When that happens, you can't find the real budget for a solution. When you avoid talking about money, you are not asking the right questions to make sure you understand the problem and help your buyer find creative ways to get the budget. Instead, they will ask for (and you will give) major discounts to create a false sense of urgency.

The Results of Your Current Belief

Belief	Mindset	Behavior	Result
"It's rude to ask about money."	Discomfort discussing money	Unable to find budget and ROI	Buyers ask for discounts

The Results of a New Belief

Belief	Mindset	Behavior	Result
"It's my responsibility to talk money."	Comfort with discussing money	Identify value of solution	Buyers are willing to pay more for value

Mindset Number 5: Fear of Rejection

Do you stop yourself from reaching out to people, or asking for the business because the first thought you have is a version of "What if they say no?" Now, what seller doesn't have to be able to handle rejection? This ability comes from your own self-image. When you are comfortable with who you are and the value that you bring, you understand that it's not you they are rejecting, it's just your offer to help. If you can't handle rejection, it will wipe you out. You may isolate yourself, feel down for days or weeks, and want to give up. When that happens, the buyers who do need and want your help will not know you exist.

The Results of Your Current Belief

Belief	Mindset	Behavior	Result
"What if they say no?"	Fear of rejection	Won't call on people or ask for business	Buyers don't know you exist

The Results of a New Belief

Belief	Mindset	Behavior	Result
"No is not the end of the world."	Ability to handle rejection	Ask more questions, or try some-one else	Buyers don't feel your desperation

Mindsets Are Not Silos

Over the past two decades, I have observed that the majority of business owners, leaders, and sellers have a combination of these sales mindsets, and that they seem to interact in unique ways. How one person reacts to an unexpected objection might be related to their need for someone to see them as smart, or to their fear of rejection. Some, when they hear buyers say they are "very interested," will get wrapped up in their thoughts and become excited about an opportunity (emotional involvement), and then worry about upsetting the buyer if they ask tough questions (approval seeking).

My observations were backed by a 2018 data analysis from Dave Kurlan, founder of OMG. "For most salespeople with more than one major weakness along with the tendency to become emotional," he writes, "the emotions weakness is triggered as part of a chain reaction... and nearly all of the weakest salespeople... have these weaknesses (and more), and the first weakness almost always triggers the second weakness."

Belief → Mindset → Behavior → Result

If you had to guess which of these sales mindsets were the top three most common weaknesses, which would you think they are? Would it be the inability to control emotions, the need for approval, a non-supportive buy cycle, discomfort with discussing money, or the fear of rejection? Write down your answer here. (No peeking to what follows!)

1 ______________________________

2 ______________________________

3 ______________________________

I had you make this guess not to quiz you, but because the mindsets you chose are likely to be the ones *you* struggle with. Now, of the three you have listed, which *one* do you think is likely to be the one you struggle with the most? Circle it now.

This is where I encourage you to start. When you read about the three most common mindsets that block sales success, pick one mindset at a time to focus on—the one that shows up the most. Do the exercises and know this: it's just the beginning.

Sales is not only a numbers game; it's a mental game.

Sales is not only a numbers game; **it's a mental game.**

Start Your Mindset Shift

When you do the exercises in this chapter, you are taking a cognitive behavioral approach to your sales mindsets. The goal of cognitive behavioral therapy (CBT) is to help change negative mindsets and, therefore, behaviors. Robert L. Leahy, director of the American Institute for Cognitive Therapy, has authored and edited twenty-seven books on cognitive behavior, and serves on several scientific committees on cognitive behavioral therapy. Leahy writes that there are several steps and approaches in the CBT framework to shift these thoughts and mindsets. Here are a few that are relevant to our exercises:

1. **When does it happen?** When does this type of thinking show up for you in your day-to-day? What is the situation, circumstance, or environment that causes you to feel or think in a certain way? Once you identify what event causes it, then you can start to examine it and create a strategy for yourself to work through it. Awareness is the first step to making a change.
2. **What is the impact?** What happens when you let this mindset take over? What are the advantages or disadvantages? How is that working out for you?
3. **What is the first thought you have about this?** What is the negative thought that repeats itself?
4. **What does the thought mean to you?** Does it mean you are a bad person or a good one? The meaning of the thought is what is driving it. Is there is any truth to the thought?
5. **What is the double standard?** If someone else did this, or said that, would you think the same about them as you do about yourself? As their supportive best friend, what advice

would you give them? Would you say they are bad? Or would you be more tolerant? Why would you be more tolerant of others than you would be of yourself?

6 **What does this mindset prevent you from?** What could you do anyway? When you put things in a big-picture perspective, it can be easier to let them go. For example, if someone doesn't like you, does that stop you from doing what you need to?

7 **How will you feel about this later?** Of course you are going to be upset in the moment, but over time our emotions and thoughts change and we gain a new perspective on it. Years from now, how will you look back at this?

In addition to reframing your thoughts and mindsets, I will ask you to do things. Sometimes scary things. But all in the name of practice.

Practice isn't about doing something perfectly, it's more about exposing yourself to your fears a little bit at a time. By practicing the techniques, you will start to shift these mindsets in your personal life, which will lead into your sales conversations. In his book *Atomic Habits*, James Clear writes that when we are trying to change our behaviors, we are more likely to stick with it when we build small habits over time.

This is work that you will do over a period, depending on how much you have to do. You may find that when you feel you have it under control, something happens to bring it back up again. That is okay, and—again—normal. The goal here is not to eliminate and cure, but to recognize and start on the path to manage and alter it.

Now, what are the three most common mindsets that get in the way of selling with your buyers (not *to* them)? In descending order of severity, they are: (1) a non-supportive buy cycle,

(2) emotional involvement, and (3) approval seeking. When you do the daily work to alter these mindsets, it will become much easier to change your approach and messaging skills with buyers.

When you want to change your habits and behaviors, I recommend you pick one and focus on making it routine. For example, if you can do something daily for fifteen minutes, that is ideal. If that doesn't seem doable, try for every other day, or once a week, or reduce the time to five minutes. The more often you do it, the faster your mindset shift can happen.

Throughout this book, I will guide you through several exercises, starting now. In fact, you have already begun. You're doing some of the work here in this book, but there is more learning waiting for you in the **Buyer First Workbook**, including a folder of worksheets and templates that can help you start to dig into your process and strategy. Go to **bit.ly/buyerfirstworkbook** to get it.

Once you have downloaded your Workbook, open "**Get Your Head in the Game—Action Plan**." You will see that there are two tables that each have four sections: Result (Buyer actions), Behavior (Your actions), Sales Mindsets (How you see things), and Beliefs (What you believe). There are two tables so that you can identify the negative result and corresponding behaviors, mindsets, and beliefs that cause it, as well as the positive ones you want to develop. This contrast is to help you see the gap in your results and how the replacement of supportive beliefs, mindsets, and behaviors leads to the results you desire.

Put another sticky note on this page so you can come back and write down the number one mindset you want to work on in order to develop the skill set that will help you sell better with your buyers.

Result: What buyer behaviors are you experiencing in your conversations?

___

Behavior: What actions or behaviors of yours could be causing that buyer behavior?

___

Sales Mindset: Which mindset, or way of seeing things, is causing your behavior?

___

Belief: What is the repeating belief that is contributing to that sales mindset?

___

As you read the following sections, come back to this page and choose the first mindset that you want to work on, and which impact or symptom you see happening in your sales conversations or process. Then choose one of the strategies that you will put into practice. In the next section, you will identify the beliefs you have about this, their impact, and how you will counter that impact.

A Non-Supportive Buy Cycle

When my youngest started his first job in a retail store, I was excited for him. His first sales job!

After the first week, he came home and complained about the people who would come in, try something on, love it, but put it back because they might find something better somewhere else. Then they would come back a few hours or days later to buy what they originally wanted. If you want it, and you have the money, why wouldn't you just buy it? That's what he would do.

We laughed a little about it, then I told him that he could be an excellent salesperson someday. He looked at me funny and asked, "What does how other people buy have to do with me being an excellent salesperson?"

I'll tell you what I told him: How you buy is how you sell.

Those who spend hours researching, comparing, and negotiating price have what is called a non-supportive buy cycle, which is the most powerful and the most common mindset weakness: 73 percent of sellers struggle with it. How you buy is how you expect other people to buy, and therefore that's how you sell. If you are someone who does a lot of research, haggles on price for no reason, or shops around to find the perfect thing or the lowest price, then you are more likely to accept it when your buyers want to do the same thing. A non-supportive buy cycle is a bad form of empathy with the procrastinators, price shoppers, comparison shoppers, researchers, and price objectors who stop and start, stall, put off, outright lie, make excuses, and tell us sad stories. Whatever the reason given, we agree with it and spend a lot of wasted time following up.

When we can make better buying decisions faster ourselves, we are better able to help our buyers do the same. If you won't push back or ask more questions when they want to think it over or compare more proposals or features, it will affect your ability to get new business and it will lengthen your sales cycle unnecessarily.

Why do we have such a hard time making decisions? Research from Mark Leary and his colleagues at Duke University suggests that a lack of "intellectual humility"—in other words, our fear of being wrong—is what paralyzes us. We feel as if we lose out on other options by choosing one. What if we make the wrong choice? Those who are willing to be proven wrong are willing to accept other perspectives and make decisions faster. When we own, embrace, share, and learn from our mistakes, we are more willing to make decisions without endless analysis and worry.

Symptoms of a Non-Supportive Buy Cycle

Of course, how you buy does depend on what you are buying. Purchasing a t-shirt is much different from buying a car, or a home. How do you know if your buying process is non-supportive? Think about the last few purchases you made (outside of a major investment such as a car or house) and ask yourself these questions:

- **Do you struggle with making a final decision?** Do you need to ask everyone's opinion? Do you delay the decision for fear of making the wrong choice? I once knew someone who was late to almost everything because they couldn't decide which socks to wear. Yes, socks! Your inability to decide makes you vulnerable to prospects who can't make decisions. You will endure their delays and excuses, which makes the time it takes to get a new customer much longer than necessary.

- **Do you need to always get the lowest price or a discount?** Some people believe that not getting some type of discount makes you a fool. One of my husband's friends prides himself on always getting a discount. Any time he purchases a new tool or toy, my husband says with utmost sarcasm: "And guess what—he got the deal of the century!" When that friend started his own training business, he would complain about people who kept trying to "low-ball" him.

Your need to shop for the lowest price makes you vulnerable to prospects who want to pay the lowest price. You may find yourself doing a lot of extra work for less money.

- **When you find what you want, do you feel the need to continue to look for comparables?** This makes you vulnerable to prospects who will talk with multiple vendors. You'll find yourself playing the comparison game with your buyer and making your sales cycle longer.

- **Is $100 a lot of money to you?** The sense that a relatively small amount of money is a lot makes you sympathize with the prospect who says, "That's expensive!" You will be more likely to discount your value and, in turn, make less money because you feel the need to justify every line item of your invoice to them.

Which of these resonates with you? Write it down here:

___

Now, when does it happen—what is the event, circumstance, or situation that causes you to think and behave this way?

I struggle with this when:

___

The impact that has is:

___

The thought I have when that happens is:

___

That means:

____

What is the double standard? What does it prevent you from doing, or how does it make you feel?

____

Now, this isn't to say you should go out and make impulsive purchases without thinking about it. It does mean that you will need to develop new supportive buying habits.

Build Better Buying Habits

While a non-supportive buy cycle is the most powerful mindset weakness, the good news is that it is the easiest one to shift.

The next time you must make a purchase decision, start with a clear picture of what you want. What are the most important and necessary features? Think of it as if you were shopping on Amazon and you needed to filter through the thousands of options displayed. What size, color, and cost range is important? In that moment, write it down, and try to keep your most important criteria to three.

When you limit your options, you eliminate the distraction of so many choices. Instead of filtering endlessly through so many possibilities, you can focus on what matters. By deciding what you need before you start your research, you keep your mind from getting overwhelmed and freezing up. It's the difference between an eight-page menu at Cracker Barrel and a one-page menu at a bed and breakfast.

As with most mindset and behavior changes, you are more likely to succeed in the long term when you start small. While this strategy can work for larger purchases, I recommend starting with something that has little risk. For example, the next time you go out for dinner, challenge yourself to choose your dish in less than two minutes and don't ask anyone else what they are having. When you shop for a major purchase, limit yourself to three options to choose from and set a deadline.

You will read several times in this book about the importance of a self-awareness and mindfulness practice, and it applies here too. In a 2013 study, researchers Andrew Hafenbrack, Zoe Kinias, and Sigal Barsade found that fifteen minutes of mindfulness meditation can help people make smarter choices by counteracting deep-rooted tendencies. The brief period of mindfulness allows people to consider the information available in the present moment, which leads them to make better decisions that lead to positive outcomes in the future.

Which strategy will you put into practice to develop a supportive buying process? Write it down now.

To make better buying decisions, I will:

____

I will practice this by:

____

When You Are Unable to Stay in the Moment

Throughout high school, college, and sometimes for fun I waited tables and did other jobs at restaurants. And while I learned a lot from those experiences, the one that stuck with me most was how we had to communicate.

If you haven't worked in a restaurant before, it's barely controlled chaos. Frantic prep work starts several hours before anyone walks in the door. Despite all that prep, there are constant changes, at an incredibly fast pace, with sometimes hostile people. (Hangry = Hungry + Angry, and it is as real as road rage, my friends.)

One busy Saturday night, when there was a line of people out the door, one of my tables ordered a hamburger and fries, but without onions. They were highly allergic to onions. (You can tell where this is going, right?) I wrote down the order, made a note to not include onions, and delivered it to the kitchen. When the chef read the order and repeated it back to me, I replied: "Yes. Oh, and the burger is without onions, though." And then left the kitchen to get their drinks.

Twenty minutes later, I brought their order to the table and my poor guest immediately started coughing. Steaming grilled onions were piled all over his burger. As he ran out of the restaurant, I stormed into the kitchen and yelled, "I told you no onions!"

Bewildered, the chef shot back: "Did you hear me repeat it back to you? How do you know I heard it? I've got five people barking orders at me and stuff burning on the grill."

I hadn't confirmed. I had no idea. The chef and I had each been so wrapped up in what we needed to do that we never stopped for a millisecond to confirm what the other person had heard—or did not hear. As a result, someone else suffered for it.

This happens in sales conversations every day. We (and our buyers) are so wrapped up in what we need to hear, strategizing in our minds about what to say or not say next, that we miss the important details. We are not in the same moment with the other person. We become time travelers, moving into the future or getting stuck in the past.

The ability to stay in the moment and manage our emotions in a conversation is the second most common weakness among salespeople, according to OMG research. Because mindsets are not silos, this weakness has an exponential impact. For a business owner who sells, this is more difficult. After all, our business is our baby, our life's work, and how we feed ourselves and our loved ones. Of course it's emotional!

I can remember times when I cared more about someone's problem (that I felt I could solve) than they did. I would wear my emotional involvement as a badge to prove that I was passionate about what I did. The truth was that I cared about how it impacted me.

For salespeople in a company, the pressure of quotas and managers constantly asking what will close next can cause emotional involvement in the outcomes. As a result, we miss the cues from our buyers that would enable us to ask better questions in the moment.

When we are overly emotional, talking to ourselves or waiting to hear something we can pounce on to pitch our solution, we are not actively listening. That makes it very hard for buyers to trust us. And impossible for us to understand them.

In the 2021 LinkedIn B2B survey, participants reported that the number one trait they want from sellers is the ability to actively listen. When we feel listened to and heard, it helps us build trust with others. Think about the last time you tried to have a conversation with someone who was looking at their phone—did you feel heard, valued, and understood?

The hidden side effect of not actively listening is that we miss important details in what our buyers say, as the chef did with me. In a recent coaching livestream, I had five participants try to sell me on their solution. I dropped key phrases and clues specifically for them to pick up on and dig into, but most missed them. Instead, they went right into talking about how they solve for the problem *they* assumed I had. This was after I had given them instructions on how to actively listen! They were so nervous going into the competition, in front of everyone, that they were still talking to themselves.

And isn't that how our sales conversations go? We are nervous, unsure of what will happen, and not fully there. Your buyers are leaving clues for you, sometimes unconsciously, but if the voice in your head is too loud, you will not hear them. You will forget what question to ask, or—worse—read your questions off your checklist, interrogation style.

Do you get excited when suspected buyers express interest in your offering? Or frustrated and angry when they push off a decision or start looking at the competition? What about when they ask you unexpected questions—do you find yourself lost in your mind as you frantically search for the answer? Do you often miss what someone says because you are talking to yourself internally?

If you answered yes to any of these things, or if they happen more often than you would care to admit, you are not alone. Sixty-three percent of sales professionals struggle to manage their emotions while selling with their buyers, according to data from OMG. Once you can better manage your emotions in the moment, it opens you up to ask the questions that will help you understand the objections, questions, and concerns your buyers have, and where they are coming from. Once that is understood, what to do with it becomes more clear.

Remember that these selling mindsets do not operate in silos. One can feed off another in debilitating combinations.

Michael Douglas (no, not the actor!) was the only salesperson for a small environmental technology company, and he was under pressure to increase his sales. When he came to me for coaching, he felt that doubling his sales in a year was a lofty goal. (You'll have to wait until chapter 9 to see how it went for him.)

Michael took his OMG sales evaluation, and it revealed to him that he was struggling to manage his emotions during sales conversations. Because he was talking to himself in his head, he wasn't actively listening to his buyers. If his buyers brought up an objection or a tough question, he was in his head scrambling on how to answer to defend his position. When they expressed interest, he was adding up the deal number in his mind.

As Michael started to become more aware of his emotions in the moment, he found that he still struggled to ask the questions that would help him understand the objections his buyers presented to him. Because he had done an evaluation of his strengths and weaknesses, he knew that his own need for approval was getting in the way of asking the questions he knew he should ask but seemed to keep avoiding in the moment. People pleasing impacts you not only when you are prospecting, but throughout the process with your buyer.

Symptoms of Not Being in the Moment

How do you know if this happens to you? The fastest way is to record your conversations and listen to them. What did you miss in the conversation? What clues got left behind from your buyers that you wished you had picked up on?

Outside of listening to your calls, you can recognize the symptoms in your daily life. Here are a few to look for:

- Do you get bored easily?
- Do you worry a lot?
- Does your mind race at night?
- After driving, are you often not able recall how you got to your destination?
- Can you remember the last thing you ate?
- Are your thoughts all about what will happen, not what is happening now?
- Can you remember people's names?
- Are you always looking for a distraction? (Otherwise known as screen addiction.)

How many of these have you noticed in the past week, or month? Write down the number below, and then write down how often you feel unable to stay in the moment.

____

Now, what is happening that causes you to think or behave this way? Write it below.

I struggle to stay in the moment when:

____

The impact that has is:

____

The thought I have when that happens is:

____

That means:

____

What is the double standard? What does it prevent you from doing, or how does it make you feel?

____

Staying in the moment when everything around you seems hard and frustrating is unpleasant. It's a natural reaction to avoid the present when dealing with stress and anxiety. But opting out is not a real option. Not if you want to connect with your buyers to better understand them and build trust.

Build Daily Strategies to Better Stay in the Moment

How can you manage your emotions and become a better active listener?

Tomas Chamorro-Premuzic is a professor at University College London and Columbia University and an associate at Harvard's Entrepreneurial Finance Lab. In his book *Why Do So Many Incompetent Men Become Leaders?*, he writes about the crucial role mindfulness has on active listening and why it is so difficult to do when society rewards us for our self-promotion. He states that, if you want to be a better listener, research suggests that you work on four areas: focus, empathy, self-control, and inclusion.

One way to do that is to counteract stress. Stress is a big trigger for us to become overly emotional. Unfortunately for us, being in sales or owning and running a business are among the top things that can cause stress. And it is a killer—literally. Countless medical studies show the impact that stress has on our health, from depression and anxiety to cancer. Managing your stress levels will have a direct impact on your ability to manage your emotions in the moment.

The most common advice you will hear about stress management is to practice meditation. The reason you hear this so often is because it works. In a 2011 Harvard Medical School study by Britta Hölzel and her colleagues, participants who did eight weeks of meditation showed changes in the areas of the brain having to do with decision making and emotional management.

I always found meditation to be difficult. I had too many thoughts running through my mind, and the idea of sitting still for any length of time seemed a waste. Then I discovered an app called Insight Timer that helps me choose what type of meditation I need and makes it easy to follow, with five- or ten-minute session options.

Because sitting still is so hard for me, I start by getting some exercise first to expend all that pent-up energy. Whether it's a fifteen-minute daily walk or a twenty-minute yoga session, exercise can go a long way to reducing stress and our ability to regulate our emotions.

If you find yourself anxious or with the jitters, try to limit your caffeine. Of course, we drink caffeine for the energy, but if you are feeling nervous or anxious then it will only increase your anxiety by affecting your sleep. That alone will make it harder for you to stay in the moment and regulate your emotions.

Another simple way to stay in the moment is to slow down. How many times have you frantically looked for your keys as you rushed out the door? I have learned that, when this happens to me, I need to stop, close my eyes, and take a breath. Usually, when I reopen my eyes my keys appear—or I remember where I left them—as if by magic.

Slowing yourself down will help you focus on one thing at a time. Multi-tasking is not a real thing. In fact, a 2021 study by Karen Murphy and Olivia Creux published in *Computers in Human Behavior* suggests that it not only distracts you, it lowers your IQ as well. Trying to do too many things at once increases our stress and takes us out of the present moment. The enemy of focus is distraction. Eliminate as many distractions as you can throughout your day, starting with turning off your email and social media notifications.

In chapter 3, I told you about the Questions and Periods Game. Not only is that exercise great for getting used to asking more questions, it also helps you develop your active listening skills. You won't know what next clarifying question to ask if you were not paying close attention to what the person you are speaking with said in the first place.

Which strategy will you put into practice to help you stay in the moment?

To stay in the moment, I will:

____

The way I will practice this is:

____

As with most of the work in this book, this is yet another area where the progress you see will be evident in your personal life as well. When I turned off email and social media notifications, I felt less anxious and stressed during the day. I was able to focus and found I could complete tasks much faster than before. Without my phone in my hand all the time, I got into fewer arguments with my husband because I was listening to him and understood his perspective better.

Being more in the present will help you build trust with your buyers, become closer to those around you, and simply enjoy your days more.

Approval Seeking

Michael had a big meeting coming up. After practicing his conversation through role-play with me, he felt ready to go, with his boss in tow. They were meeting with two senior managers from a $22 billion a year company. Prior to the meeting, he had established an agenda with them. He used their words, not his, and knew exactly what they wanted to talk about. They had given him a list of six things to discuss. To kick off the meeting, he asked them where they wanted to start. Here is how Michael later told me the conversation went:

"Let's start here," the most senior manager said, indicating an item.

"Okay, why do we want to start there?" Michael asked.

The manager replied, "Well, I guess because it's first on the list."

"Is it the most important?"

"Well, it's all important," the manager shot back.

"Okay, so help me out here," Michael said. "If you were to rank this low, medium, or high in terms of value, where would it fall?"

"I don't know. Low to medium."

Michael paused for the elephant in the room. It was huge. He shared with me later that the old him might not have addressed it and instead would have moved forward with what the senior manager had asked. The new Michael had a tiny Carole on his shoulder that he could imagine smacking him across his head. He knew what he needed to say but wasn't sure how, and was nervous that he would upset his buyer by challenging him. But he faced his need to be liked and did it anyway.

"You don't know me very well. But if you decide you want to know me better after today, you will learn I am a very transparent guy. I have a question, but I am afraid to cross the line. If I ask it, and you think I crossed the line, will you tell me?"

Michael told me later that he was sure no one had ever set up a question to this man in that way, because the executive gave him a puzzled look through his glasses and replied, "Well, I am a transparent guy too, so yeah, I'll tell you. What's your question?"

"You don't seem to be the type of guy that flies by the seat of his pants. You have two hours scheduled with us today. You have brought in your team. Why would you commit that amount of time and resources to something that is a low to medium priority?"

Michael pinpointed that as the moment when the meeting changed. The executive informed him that the first agenda item was a low to medium to him, but a medium to high for his team. "But that one," he said, pointing to the third agenda item, "the CEO is on me to fix it. That's my highest priority right now."

Michael won the opportunity to move to the next stage with that company. More than that, his boss was floored. He had never seen anyone do that before. Michael didn't know it at the time, but that meeting changed his boss's view of him, and set him on a path to become VP of sales for the company only a few years later.

An unchecked need for approval will prevent you from asking the tough questions in your journey to sell with your buyer. When that happens, you will not fully understand the cost of their problem and the compelling reason for them to make a change. Maybe you think of the question, but chicken out because you are afraid it will upset them. Perhaps you know you need to talk to their boss, but don't want them to feel as if you are going around them. As a result, the person you had a "good conversation with" doesn't return your calls and emails. Or, they ask for a steep discount. Asking tough questions is what your buyers want you to do, and what you need to do to win their respect and trust.

Symptoms of a High Need for Approval

Seeking the approval of others is something we learn from infancy. When we did something, we looked to others to see if we did it right. We evolved as a civilization by forming tribes and communities; whether others liked you could mean your very survival.

This is normal human behavior.

How do you know if your need for approval is getting in your way? Ask yourself these questions:

- Do you feel guilty for setting boundaries with others, or for saying no?
- When others do not recognize your hard work or overachievement, do you feel upset?

- Do you need someone else to validate your decisions before you can move forward?
- Do you hate being alone? Or do you jump from one relationship to another without stopping to consider what happened in the last one?
- Are you unable to disagree with others or challenge them when they are wrong, because you don't want to be judged, singled out, or to go against the group?
- Are you constantly comparing yourself (and your achievements) to others?
- Do you punish yourself when you don't win or get chosen? Do you replay it over and over to find every little flaw that caused it?

How many of these ring true for you? The more honest you are with yourself, the more you might recognize some of these behaviors. We all do them at one time or another. But if you find yourself saying yes to a lot of these questions, then your need for approval is getting in the way of your sales success.

Start the mindset shift now by identifying the situation where your behavior or thought comes up. Write that down here. Or, if none of those questions exactly ring true for you, write down what does ring true.

My need for approval happens when:

____

The impact that has is:

____

The thought I have when that happens is:

___

That means:

___

What is the double standard? What does it prevent you from doing, or how does it make you feel?

___

The problem arises when these tendencies carry over into our sales role. Sixty percent of sellers struggle with a need for approval, making it the third most common mindset weakness. It prevents us from being able to ask the tough questions that help our buyers think differently, like Michael did. That in turn keeps us from uncovering the true nature and impact of the problem, and the compelling reason for our buyer to make a change. Which then leads to heavily discounted and delayed opportunities—or buyers you never hear from again.

Build Strategies to Curb the Need for Approval

How do we manage the very human aspect of seeking approval and validation from others in our sales conversations so that we can ask the tough questions that challenge our buyer's way of thinking about their problem and solutions? Here are a few strategies to choose from.

First, limit the time you spend scrolling social media. Comparison is the death of joy. No one ever won a race by looking sideways. Their path is not your path; their goals are not your goals. I could quote a dozen more clichés here. But have you ever considered that the other people in those social media accounts might be comparing themselves to you? If they aren't, I can guarantee that someone is. You are unique in your strengths and experiences, and besides—who shows the mess of their lives on social media?

You can start this now by tracking how much time you spend scrolling social. Whatever the number is, tomorrow focus on spending fifteen minutes less. Or, pick a time in the day where you won't pick up your phone—maybe it's your lunch break, or dinner time. If you must, put your phone in another room where you can't reach it.

Next, be more kind to the person in the mirror. Reducing your social media scroll time may make it easier to replace some of your negative self-talk as well. When you hear yourself beating yourself up, stop, pause, and replace the thought with something positive and supportive. For example, when I struggled with my own sales in my business, I would often find myself saying, "I suck at this. I will never figure it out!" So, I would replace that repeating thought with: "I am not good at this—yet. But I am smart enough to figure it out."

Finally, say no more often. If you have a hard time saying no when you want to, make the extra effort. You don't have to start with your boss—there are more low-risk ways you could practice this. Maybe it's when your spouse suggests a movie you don't care for, or a friend asks you to drop everything to go out, or when your kids ask you to drive them somewhere. It could be someone who asks you to do something for free. It might be when a buyer asks you to do something that's not in your area of expertise.

When we say yes to everything and never push back or set boundaries, it's natural for others to wonder what we stand for—if anything. If you think back to the research from the previous chapter, you'll recall that buyers place more trust in those who can challenge their thinking and approach to a problem. When I said no to my sister's boss Jack and advised him to hire the better qualified candidate for what he needed, that was the moment I earned his trust. All I had to do was say no.

It can be hard to know how to say no. The next time you are faced with it, try this: "That sounds incredible, but right now I am focused on X. That means I will have to pass."

Which strategy will you put into practice to help curb your need for approval in your life?

To begin reining in my need for approval, I will:

____

I will practice this by:

____

When you employ this or any of the other strategies I provide here in small ways in your everyday life, there are going to be times when you need validation. That is okay—just make sure the person you are seeking validation from is safe and won't use it against you later.

And that brings me to why it is important to actively build your supportive network. To address your high need for approval is a deep-rooted behavior change. It's scary to do something new, and it's natural to seek validation that we are doing it right. When you have an accountability group that gives you advice, and that enables you to give your advice, it will help you build your confidence in your abilities, and in the changes you want to make.

As a business owner, I was fortunate to have a group of other women sales experts who did exactly that. When I first made the transition to sales from my marketing agency, I was full of doubts and as a result I clung to unhealthy relationships for too long. The day that Lori Richardson invited me to coffee and told me about her group—Women Sales Pros—I was still doubtful. But the relationships there helped me see clearly how my own need for approval was crushing me and my sales success. Seek out groups for business owners and sellers that can act as a trusted accountability partner for you. If you can't find one locally, join the online Buyer First Community on Facebook at bit.ly/buyerfirstbookclub.

We have your back.

Put Your Oxygen Mask on First

Remember, one of the most important things you can do to improve your sales results is your own self-care. As Jeanette Bronée writes in her book *The Self-Care Mindset*, when you use your mind to work better for you, you harness your own ability to change and grow.

Your daily work on the mindsets that hold you back from sales success will be a constant evolution. As you recognize and overcome the events, situations, and circumstances that cause them to flare up (yes, as if they were a bad rash), you may find that some will be replaced by other, usually less severe, triggers.

When my husband took a 50 percent pay cut to change careers right when my business was taking off, it was something I knew could cause some money-related mindsets for me. *What if we end up back where we were before and not able to buy groceries? Am I making the right decisions in taking these risks right now?*

The times when large opportunities came my way acted as an event as well. *I'm not smart enough, experienced enough, credible enough for them to work with me. Who do I think I am?* Relying on my support system and preparing for these thoughts with every strategy and tool I had learned is what got me through it, as it will for you if you are open and aware. Make the strategies, habits, and techniques in this chapter part of

Be more kind
to the person
in the mirror.

your daily routines. You know that to keep weight off you must change your lifestyle rather than simply try a diet for a while and then go back to your old ways; it's likewise true that to build a foundation of successful selling with your buyers, you must strengthen your ability to actively listen and ask great questions. The exercises described in these pages are designed to help you manage the non-supportive mindsets that could get in the way of that.

You now know how to identify the beliefs that become the mindsets that lead to the sales behaviors you can change so you can reach your results with buyers.

Sounds simple, doesn't it? It is—but not always easy. It might be the most difficult thing you will do. Your beliefs about sales started long ago and have become a part of who you are. You are not going to change them overnight.

But if I can do it, you can do it.

Yes, it is hard work, but consider the upside. When you start to change what and how you think, it will not only impact your ability to sell and get more customers or clients—it is a process that will impact nearly every aspect of your life.

During the process to become a better seller, you will become a better human.

When I began the work on my own sales mindsets, it not only changed how I interacted with my buyers, but it also changed how I showed up for my family and friends. I realized this when my kids told me, "You yell a lot less now, Mom."

When you focus on shifting the mindsets that keep you from being in the present moment, cause you to seek external validation unnecessarily, delay your decisions, make you uncomfortable talking about money, and cause rejection to wipe you out and hinder you from doing what you know you should, you are taking big steps forward to sell with your buyers.

KEY ACTIONS AND TAKEAWAYS

Mindset trumps skill set. There are five sales-specific mindsets that will impact your ability to sell with your buyers. Everyone struggles with them, but you can develop your own system and process to address these hidden weaknesses through awareness and daily self-care.

Start small by choosing one mindset to shift, make note of the impact it has, and commit to one daily habit that you will adopt to start making incremental changes to your sales mindsets.

5

FIND YOUR PEOPLE

Go out on a limb. That's where the fruit is.

ATTRIBUTED TO JIMMY CARTER

WHEN YOU HEAR the word "prospecting," what images and actions come to mind?

Do you think of vendors standing in their booths, calling out to you? Does the thought of cold calling make you cringe? Do you recall memories of your last uncomfortable networking conversation?

In case you haven't figured it out yet in this book, you are not alone. Thirty-one percent of professional sellers struggle with finding new business, according to Objective Management Group. The constant need to find new people to talk to can be mentally exhausting—because we make it more complicated than it needs to be.

My kids love to remind me of the time that I had to pick them up from school early because of an incoming blizzard. Because it was a forty-five-minute drive one way, I planned to use the hour and half there and back to do my prospecting calls with my Bluetooth attached to my ear.

The kids piled into the car, and as we drove, I made several calls, leaving a voicemail message when they didn't pick up. The snow was getting deeper outside, but we were almost home, and I had only one call left to make. *You must hustle to get new business*, I thought. *And if this is what it takes, this is what I'll do.*

Ring.

"Hello, this is Ken."

Oh crap, he answered! I waved frantically at the kids to shush, using my best wide-eyed stern mom look.

"Hi Ken, this is Carole Mahoney, from Mahoney Internet Marketing. How are you today? I am calling because I offer online marketing services for small businesses so they can get more customers from their website. I do everything from social media to SEO to email marketing to Google Analytics. My Think, Do, Review framework will grow your business because people will be able to find you better than any Yellow Pages ad..."

"Yeah, I'm gonna have to stop you right there. We don't have a website right now. Thanks for calling."

"Oh, you don't have a website? That's great, because I do that too. How are you getting customers now?"

I don't remember what Ken said after that, because my car was no longer moving forward; in fact, we had slid sideways and backward down the hill in front of our house.

With the kids shouting, "Mom, Mom, MOM!" and the dog barking in the hatch behind them, I told Ken I would call him right back.

Fifteen minutes later, with the kids safely in the house, I called Ken back and got his voicemail. *Maybe I need a better voicemail script?*

This chapter may be the whole reason you bought this book. Maybe because you want to avoid this scenario (who wouldn't?), or maybe because you want to know how to make an exchange like this go your way. I can't tell you how many times I used to think, "If someone could tell me what I need to do and promise me that it'll work, then I will do it!"

How many books, podcasts, and other pieces of content have you consumed with that same goal? How many acronyms have you followed in a process that brought you marginally different results? And how often did you find a reason why it wouldn't work for you? Just because we know what to do doesn't mean we will do it. We know that eating more vegetables and getting more exercise is how we get healthy, but how many of us do? In that, and this, our mindsets and thought patterns get in the way.

That is why we started with working on your mindsets in the previous chapter before we got into what actions you need to take with buyers. Now that you are more aware of the mindsets and beliefs that you need to work on to successfully sell with your buyer, it's time to get into your buyer's head and learn everything you can about them.

Dive Into Your Buyer's World

Being relevant to your buyers will require research. The challenge is that, in our minds, we don't think we have the time. The urgency to get people talking causes us to skip over this incredibly important (albeit sometimes boring) task.

Take Charlie, for example. He's a business development rep (BDR) who was frustrated over the level of activities he had to do to get enough meetings booked. When he came to me for coaching, he admitted that the way he had been doing things was burning him out. He had all the automated email sequences to send that he was constantly tweaking based on what other BDRs said worked for them, did more outreach than anyone else on his team, and yet had the least number of meetings booked and lowest monthly recurring revenue.

He couldn't possibly do more activity—there wasn't enough time in the day—but the idea of slowing down and doing research to personalize his approach more seemed counterintuitive. If he wasn't getting enough meetings and revenue in now, how was doing less outreach going to help?

After several weeks of coaching, he was frustrated enough to finally follow my advice. One day he got on our coaching call and his voice cracked—he sounded like he was teary eyed. When he said he wanted me to listen to a call recording, I felt worried about what I was about to hear. "Is this a good call?" I asked. He assured me that it was, and fast-forwarded the recording to the end of the call. The sales rep he had set the meeting for was planning next steps with the VP of sales when he was interrupted.

"Look, I can't tell you how many cold calls and emails I get from BDRS trying to book a meeting with me. Over the four and a half years I have been in this role, I have ignored them all. I wasn't considering your solution, but when Charlie reached out it was obvious that he had done his homework and had crafted a relevant message based on that. That is the only reason I took this meeting—because he hit on something I hadn't thought of. I don't know who has been training him, but I wanted to let you know that kudos are in order."

Charlie was so relieved that his hard work had paid off that he was nearly in tears. Less than twelve months later, Charlie helped land the largest deal in his department out of 130 other BDRS.

But that moment was the first time he believed he could do this.

And you can do it too.

Think of your research as the map you take on a trip. I am old enough to remember having to use paper maps to get to a new place. First you had to get the right map; a national map isn't much help when you are on Commercial Street in Portland, Maine, and need to get to St. James Street in Boston,

Massachusetts. You need a map of New England roadways because that is the relevant map for your specific journey. Or, if you want to get techy, setting your Google Maps to show you driving routes isn't going to help much when you are hiking Zion National Park.

As you go through your own journey with your buyers, they will be the ones who navigate the rest of the journey with you. First, you must meet them where they are. To do that, you are going to have to do a bit of detective work. Here's how you find the clues that will tell you how to start the journey with your buyer.

Mapmaking

To start this step, visit **bit.ly/buyerfirstworkbook** and download the **Buyer First Workbook** folder (if you haven't already). When you have the files, open the one called "**Find Your People Workbook.**" Now it's time to find out where your buyers are, so you can meet them there.

How well do you know what your buyer's day-to-day is, or the challenges they face? Do you know something they don't know? If not, then it's time to educate yourself so you can find the data that is relevant to them, pull an insight that they may not have considered, and ask the questions that go deeper into their goals, challenges, and perceived options.

Where to start is the hardest part of anything. The rabbit-hole-time-suck called the internet makes it more difficult because there is so much information out there. (Which is how your buyers feel too.) What information matters, and what is the best way to use it to be buyer first in all of your interactions? How do you know which map is the right place to begin?

To get started with your buyer research, consider these three types of information: demographic, operational, and situational.

Demographic information is external-facing information, such as industry category, location, number of employees, amount of revenue, and job titles. This is the type of information that is easy to find on LinkedIn, using the "People Search" function. This is a good place to start building the list of contacts—people for you to reach out to later to see how you might be able to help them, or help someone they know. You may be surprised to see how many people there are.

Operational information is internal information within your buyer's company, or about them personally. It could include the type of equipment and software they use, their decision-making process and purchasing policies, the metrics they track, their organizational hierarchy, their sales process, price points, margins, regulatory compliance, and job descriptions. Some of this information can be gathered searching Google and LinkedIn, as well as through your early conversations with your prospect.

Situational information is the information about your buyer's strategies, biases and beliefs, financial status, values, mission, culture, competitors, management style, and industry changes and disruptions, along with any other environmental, cultural, or circumstantial information. Some of this can come through conversations, some through research on the internet—particularly your prospect's own websites and press releases.

When it comes to gathering these three types of information, there are two methods: quantitative (or low-touch), and qualitative (or high-touch).

Quantitative research can be done on your own through the internet. Think of this type of low-touch research as your high-level regional map that shows you the major roadways. This is where you hunt for clues to understand your buyer's world.

Qualitative research is how you use those clues. Think of it as taking the map you created through your low-touch research, and narrowing in to identify the streets you need to take. Imagine it as if your GPS has no signal, and you have to stop and ask the locals how to get somewhere. This type of high-touch research will be more time consuming because you will be one-on-one with people who are like your buyers.

Yes, that means having conversations with potential buyers—who I call "suspects"—and/or conversations with the people who can introduce you to those potential buyers. "Suspects" is a good label for them because you haven't spoken to them yet, which means you only *suspect* they might have a challenge or problem you can help with. Once you talk with them and they share a problem that you could help with, they become a prospect.

Is all research and information equally important? No, not according to Leff Bonney, research director at B2B Decision-Labs and professor of sales and marketing at the Florida State University Sales Institute. He applied his research to 6,000 opportunities at twenty different companies and found that "problem profiles and trigger events are the strongest predictors of a buyer's journey."

The goal in your research and early conversations is to understand the event that causes them to realize they have a problem, as well as what your buyers understand about their problem, what they believe is the cause of it, and whether they agree internally on the problem, its cause, and its likely solution. Now, where do you start and what do you look for in your research? Here are a few places to begin.

Google Search

To do this type of research well, you are going to have to learn how to be an efficient searcher on Google. Here are a few tips to become a pro-level web searcher:

- **Start with general search terms.** If you know where to look, kicking off your search with the most obvious and high-level words and phrases will lead you to deeper levels of terms and information. Scroll to the bottom of the first page of your search results and you will see related terms that others have searched for. This can help you narrow your search

The more you talk about what your buyers care about, **the more people you will attract.**

terms, or lead you to new ones you may not have considered that will uncover even more useful information.

- **Go wild.** The tilde (the ~ symbol) acts like a "wildcard" trigger for Google, telling the search engine to search both for the word in question and for any synonyms and keywords that are closely related to it. Type it in before your search term (for example, *~technology*) to widen your search. If you are searching for multiple words or terms at once, you can use the word *or* to include pages that include either word (for example, *technology or software*).

- **Follow the connections.** If you need to find more sources of information, you can search for links to specific websites. If you want to know what other companies are linking to a specific page of a relevant website, type *link:* before the URL—for example, *link:unboundgrowth.com*.

- **Search by site.** You can search for your terms within a specific website or type of domain name. If you typed in *behavior change site:.edu*, for example, then you would get results about behavior change on academic .edu websites.

- **Narrow in.** To drill down to specific phrases, use quotation marks around your search term (*"ROI of sales technology"*) to find information that uses that exact phrase. You may need to exclude words from your search to get more relevant results. To do this, use the minus sign. For example, searching for *ROI of sales technology -"real estate"* will show only results that do not include "real estate."

Using search tricks like these—first going wide, then focusing in tight—can uncover a goldmine's worth of insight and information that you wouldn't have come across by Googling a few common terms for the industry or sector.

Social Media

New and emerging social media platforms are a constant source of distraction. How do you know which to spend your time on? If you guessed that the answer depends on where your buyers are, then you are catching on. So, go where your buyers are! A first step to finding out where to go is to get the latest Pew Research Center Social Media Fact Sheet and look up the trends based on their demographics, such as gender, age, and location.

If you are selling a solution for businesses, then LinkedIn is the place to be. This is where you can see what your potential buyers talk about in their professional world. Plus, you can download your current list of connections on LinkedIn and use People Search to sort it by factors such as these:

- **Industry:** Which industries do you have experience or interests in, or which industries are specific to the solution you offer?
- **Job title:** Who is the person who makes the business decision for your offering? Who are the people who will be using it, or impacted by it?
- **Affiliates, associations, or group memberships:** Who do your buyers look to for information to keep them current on trends?
- **Location:** Do you operate in a certain region? Do they?

If you use LinkedIn Sales Navigator (and if your offering is to other businesses, I recommend that you do), you can search by using advanced filters such as:

- **Company headcount:** Is your solution best for a certain sized company?

- **Role function and years in current company and role:** Is your ideal buyer new to the role or industry they are in, or are they more experienced?
- **Activities and experiences:** What might you have in common with them? What do they prefer to do with non-working hours? What is important to them?
- **Keywords used in posted content:** What words will people use to describe the problem or challenge you can solve?
- **Common connections and connections of specific people:** Do you want to reach out to people who have certain connections you know in common? Or to people you have worked with in the past?

(To learn more about how to effectively use LinkedIn for research and outreach, follow this affiliate link: bit.ly/linkedinbuyerfirst.)

If your ideal buyers are individuals, the personal social media sites are your best bet. Facebook, Instagram, and TikTok are places to start. Many have similar functions; I recommend you decide what information is relevant and how you would use it before heading down that rabbit hole.

In addition to the research and list-building functionality these sites offer, many have advertising platforms. When you sign up for an account, you can do further searches to see what size audience you may be able to reach.

Industry Associations

There is an association for almost anything you can think of. There is an association for associations! Look to the associations for the industry or role of your buyers. Do you offer services for senior citizens? AARP is the go-to association for them. Maybe you want to help building managers at manufacturing companies; if so, you need to be involved with the National Association of Manufacturers. Or perhaps you are developing a new green energy technology—then you should be a member of the American Clean Power Association.

What trends are the relevant associations reporting and educating on? Who are their members? Where are they located? What are the most popular topics on the membership forums? Attend their meetings and listen to what members are talking about.

Other Research Sources

Many social media sites offer the ability for you to conduct surveys and polls to gather information and opinions from your ideal audience. You can do this with Google Forms and SurveyMonkey as well. And if you don't have a long email list or a lot of followers to share your surveys with, you can pay sites like SurveyMonkey to access their contact databases.

Job boards are another great place for information on demand for your products or services. Check the job listings on sites like LinkedIn, Indeed, Glassdoor, or Monster. What are the duties and responsibilities they list? What experience is important? This is the kind of information you should include on your own profiles, social media posts, and website. The companies that are trying to fill those roles may be open to the idea of outsourcing those roles if they are not able to find qualified candidates, and could become future clients.

Look for other clues in economic forecasts and how the current economy might impact your buyer. What government regulations are coming up that could change things for them? What mergers and acquisitions are common in their industry? What other news comes up if you search them, their company, and their industry?

If you are trying to reach people in publicly traded companies, listen to their shareholder calls and make note of the strategies and initiatives they are prioritizing. This, combined with your research into their recent and posted hires, will give you insights into what they are planning for and how you might be able to help.

Later, after you have started a conversation with your suspected buyer, you can take what they share and create a survey using the platform of your choice to expand your reach beyond those interviews. Ask your buyers if they would be willing to share the survey link with their networks, and offer to share the results with them. Once you have gained information directly from your buyers, you can turn it into a webinar or podcast as a way to collect more engaged followers for your email list and social feeds. Invite your buyers on as guests, so others in their field can learn from them. In fact, why not host a regular podcast, webinar, or some other type of free event to create a place for your buyers to talk to each other and to hear from you about the challenges and struggles you have uncovered during your conversations?

The more you talk about what your buyers care about, the more people you will attract. The question of what to say in your marketing becomes less of a mystery.

Pick Your People

Just as single people think they need to go and find their person, as business owners and salespeople we sometimes think we need to call strangers to get customers, not realizing that we already know people who could be a customer, or a referral to a customer. Sometimes it's not a matter of finding new people to talk to—it's a matter of picking someone we know, and having a new type of conversation with them.

It's true that you must be willing to reach out to strangers, but there is no reason why you can't also reach out to people you know, right now. Yes, even if your offering isn't fully formed yet. Yes, even if you're going into a new role and haven't started onboarding yet. You may already know someone who is in the same role of the person you need to help, or someone who knows someone who is. You simply need to do a bit more detective work to identify them.

It's a simple exercise to write a list of people, yet I have found that some still resist this step. If you are a seller in a company, they may have existing lists for you, or a territory with target accounts. If you don't have that, or if you work in a startup or are starting out as a business owner, then this is your first step. Get a piece of paper, create a blank document, or open the "**Find Your People Workbook**" in the **Buyer First Workbook**. Then, brain dump two lists of people:

1. **Suspects:** These are people who you suspect might have a problem. Either because you know them, or they are in the role of the person who you can help.

2. **Referrers:** These are the people who know or work with the suspects in your first list, or others like them.

Not anyone and everyone can or should be your client or customer. Specifics matter, because they enable you to see more clearly who your best-fit buyers are. Later, we will be talking about which specifics matter the most and how they help your buyers make decisions and see value in your solution.

I have been marketing my business online and in person for nearly two decades, but the majority of my clients still come from referrals and introductions. Not because marketing doesn't work or isn't necessary—it does and is—but because, from the earliest days, it has been the people who know and trust me who come to me first before seeking out other solutions. When those clients then refer me to someone else, that trust is transferred from the client to the new prospective buyer who trusted them. What to say matters less when trust is transferred.

Research by Tim Riesterer, Rob Perrilleon, and Nick Lee from B2B DecisionLabs tested various messaging frameworks to get executive decision makers involved. And while there was a clear winner in terms of which framework worked best for going directly to executive decision makers (more on that in the following chapters), they also tested those messaging frameworks when the referral came from someone on their team. The study suggests that the message doesn't matter as much when it comes from a trusted source. It appears that the executives were willing to take the meeting based on their relationship with the referrer.

When you focus your outreach efforts toward referrals and introductions, the lifetime value of the customers you win goes way up. Philipp Schmitt and Bernd Skiera from Goethe University and Christophe Van den Bulte from the Wharton School report that the lifetime value of referred customers is on average 16 percent higher than that of non-referred customers. Referrals are how B2B buyers prefer to start their buying decisions, and those opportunities are worth more.

You might be thinking, "But I don't know anyone," or, "No one knows me." I promise that could not be further from the truth. In fact, if you are early in your career, it is your lifeline. No one is an island; we all have people we know. We simply assume that those we know don't count.

I can almost hear the next thought in your head: "I don't want to put people out by asking them to introduce me to others. That would be uncomfortable for them, me, and the person they introduce."

My colleague Joanne Black is one of the leading experts on referrals and has written several books and a LinkedIn course on this type of prospecting. She has worked with hundreds of clients and companies around the world. She got into this work when she saw a problem with a client who was surveying their top fifty customers to see how happy they were. When Joanne's clients asked these best customers if they would be willing to be a referral for them, most said yes.

But no one was asking them.

Why do we dislike asking for referrals so much? According to Joanne, a lot of people think that asking for referrals seems desperate. We think, "If I were successful, I wouldn't have to ask. Having to ask means I am not successful."

It's not true, which makes this yet another mindset to address and shift. Referrals are how most of us decide who to buy from. I am a member of several local Facebook groups in my town, and most of the posts I see are people looking for someone to do X—"Who does the group recommend?" they ask.

The "who" for your list of referrers should include the circles of influence for your buyers. For example, when I wanted to work with tech startups, I found common connections with people who could act as interim sales leaders or go-to-market consultants. When it came time for their startup clients to hire a sales team, that leader or consultant could add value to their offering by referring them to me, or by bundling my offering in with theirs. If you are a bookkeeper, you could form this kind of referral relationship with accountants. Or if you are a graphic designer, you may want to seek out marketing agency owners who could include your work into their offering for their clients.

Your referrer list can include other professionals you want to meet, and it can include others you know who work with your buyers in a different capacity. This form of indirect prospecting can open doors for you that you may not have known existed.

The buyer first mindsets and frameworks apply to these conversations as well. Most importantly, when you are asking for an introduction, make it specific. Don't ask for "anyone you know"; ask for the first person who comes to mind—or, if you know the connection you want to speak with, name them. Remember that specifics make it easier for us to remember, and that applies to asking for introductions. We will dig into how to make that ask shortly.

Ask for the Meeting

Once you have done your homework, it is time to take the first step. For many, this step is the scariest one. *What if they say no and don't want to talk to me? Or, worse, what if they totally ignore me?* Remember, it's not about you. Selling isn't something you do *to* others, it is something you do *with* them.

There are many reasons why someone might say no, or not reply at all—and most have nothing to do with you. Maybe they are so busy they don't have time to talk or respond. (Busy people are, of course, the ones who need the most help to get things done.) Or they could be sick, or on vacation. Or maybe it isn't the right time.

If you are a business owner developing a solution or a seller for a company in a new role (or you have been in the role and have hit a wall) and you want to prepare for it, treat your outreach to buyers like an interview. No pitch, no ask—other than the questions you want to learn from. Here is a sample message you can try, test, and adapt to your needs:

> *Subject line:* Your thoughts and feedback on this?
>
> Hi <First Name>, can you believe it has been five years since we worked together at <business>? How are things in your world?
>
> You came to mind while I have been working on a new project involving <topic>. Would you be open to catching up and sharing some feedback on what I have been working on?
>
> Look forward to speaking with you soon!
>
> Best,
> <Your Name>

Does this seem too simple to work? Remember, people like to share their thoughts, opinions, and ideas. At this point, that is all you are looking for. You may be tempted to add in a call to action—to try to book the meeting right away. Instead, go for the micro-commitment of a response from them. Then, once they respond, ask to book a day and time.

You may still be thinking, "What if I don't know the person I want to connect with?" Yes, that's right—as I said before, you will have to approach strangers. In that situation, find something they have written or said from your research, whether that was in an interview, social post, or article, and look for some part of it that resonates with you. Then, adapt this sample messaging framework to reach out to them:

> *Subject line:* Your article on <topic> resonated with me
>
> Hi <First Name>, thank you for sharing your perspective and insights in <cite source>—your comment <"insert quote from them"> made me think differently about <topic>.
>
> I have been working on a new project involving <topic> and I wondered if you would be open to a 15-minute conversation to share your expert feedback on what I have been working on?
>
> I look forward to speaking with you soon!
>
> Best,
> <Your Name>

Now, what if they reply and say yes? Then what? Schedule a time to talk for fifteen minutes, then start coming up with your questions to ask (which we will cover in the next three chapters).

Getting that first meeting is daunting, and that is why we tend to avoid this activity. This is normal, everyday human behavior. As when you want to save money, you have to put a little bit away every day. If you don't, then you have nothing to earn interest on. But if we want to put it off, we can always find a reason why we can't. And so we find ourselves with no savings, or—in the case of prospecting—no customers coming in.

Procrastination happens to us all. Especially when the task we need to do is something we don't want to do.

How do we stop stopping ourselves?

Avoid Prospecting Procrastination

Zach was a new business development representative and would spend hours creating email sequences and scripts, religiously checking his company's Slack channel multiple times a day to find the latest question, hack, or trick to get people to agree to talk to him or take a meeting. When it came time to make calls to those people, however, Zach always put it off. He knew he needed to, but did it only when he had no other choice. And when he did get on the phone, it went horribly.

When I asked Zach what he thought prospecting was, all of his answers were about finding qualified opportunities. He kept getting stuck on the alphabet soup of sales processes. He couldn't see past what he needed to do. I challenged him to think about what he needed *before* he could get to those steps in his process. I gave him hints to guide him to the answer: before Zach can reach his outcome of a qualified opportunity, he must get a human being to respond to him.

But this seemed too simple to Zach. *It has to be more complicated than that!*

So, he was still hesitant. What should he do when people don't want to talk to him, or when they tell him they're too busy, that now isn't the time? "Isn't that exactly why you are calling them?" I asked. "Because they are busy and don't have time to figure this problem out right now?"

That got Zach thinking. But he was still uneasy with calling and interrupting people. Of course, it is scary. I invite you to think of it this way: when you see someone carrying so much stuff that they're dropping things, are you the type of person who will walk by without offering to help because they didn't ask? Or are you the type of person who will risk being rejected and offer help before they ask?

A few weeks later I got a text message from Zach: "You are not going to believe the call I just had. I got someone to laugh!"

During our coaching call later, Zach told me how he had been feeling anxious about calling people, but then remembered what I said—as if I was there whispering in his ear: "They are people, like you or me." That helped him to relax and make the calls he had researched and planned for. He didn't have a massive epiphany, and there had been no dramatic change in how people acted—*he* felt different. He was more calm, more relaxed, and—in some cases—he was even having fun on his cold calls. At one point, someone he called said they had a meeting in five minutes, and Zach responded, "Must be something going around, seems like everyone has a meeting in five minutes when I call!" This made the other person laugh—and that opened Zach's mind to the idea that he could have fun with this.

Prospects are people.

What was getting in the way of Zach's prospecting that might be in your way too?

Nearly all of us—salespeople, managers, business owners, and entrepreneurs—will admit that prospecting is necessary, and we should do more of it. But prospecting feels as if we are dating: full of the fear of rejection, the pressure to make a perfect first impression, and the uncertainty about whether or not the right person is out there. As business owners and sellers, this intimidation can make us avoid prospecting and wait for people to come to us. There are very few people in the world

Prospects
are
people.

who don't have "call reluctance." I mean, none of us wants to interrupt and upset people, and who wants to get hung up on?

I've coached and worked with business development reps and sales development reps like Zach whose job is make cold calls all day long—they have been called very explicit words, been hung up on, and felt as if they were a horrible person. But the world doesn't end, their dogs still love them, and there is someone out there who needs their help but doesn't know it yet.

Fear causes us to procrastinate the things we don't look forward to and don't want to do. We underestimate the power of procrastination when we believe we have the willpower to make it happen no matter what the obstacle is, even when the obstacle is our own discomfort. We don't take into account that the task we are about to do might be uncomfortable, and, when it is, it is easier to quit or put it off. We think, "It shouldn't be this hard. I must be doing it wrong. I should be able to do this—what is the big deal?"

Indeed, what is the big deal?

In addition to the fear of rejection and failure, another thing I have observed in myself and in my clients who struggle with procrastination is that we also grapple with a scarcity mindset. This happens when we look at the world, its resources, or our opportunities as slices in a pie. There are only so many slices to go around—once the pie is gone, it's gone. No more left. We must get as much of it for ourselves as we can before the competition does. This leads to the need for perfectionism or getting it exactly right the first time—no mistakes allowed.

Those with an abundance mindset believe that they can make more pie, and that there is plenty of pie in the world for everyone.

To break free from procrastination, reexamine your mindset, focus on abundance, and accept the fact that you're going to have some uncomfortableness involved in the task that you're about to do. You will struggle, stumble, and doubt. You may not be able to do it.

Yet.

Fear of rejection and failure are not the only reasons we put off prospecting. There are two common biases that can get in your way of reaching out to people, or doing the work in this book to reach your goals.

Present Bias

Why don't we do the things we know we should? One reason for this is what Richard Thaler, a U.S. economist and winner of the 2017 Nobel Prize in Economic Sciences for his work on behavioral economics and psychology, calls "present bias": our tendency toward immediate gratification leads us to put off any tasks that are good for our future at the cost of present enjoyment—such as saving money, eating healthy, and going to the gym. It seems so far off that it is not real.

"It's not as if one bag of potato chips is going to make me fat tomorrow."

"I have enough work and clients to get me through; I don't need to worry about prospecting right now."

"Everything is fine."

Until right now becomes next month and you realize—whoops—it takes time to get a client in. Next thing you know, you are scrambling to prospect, creating more pressure on yourself, more need to get it right because now there isn't any time for mistakes—bills are due. That roller-coaster ride of revenue will make you nauseous.

How then do we mitigate a present bias that prevents us from prospecting consistently?

You can combat this bias by working in a reward system; in other words, by creating ways to make those tasks more instantly gratifying.

Try this: put a block of time—anywhere from twenty to forty-five minutes—on your calendar tomorrow or in the next few days to do the prospecting exercises in this chapter. Right after that, schedule a reward. Maybe it's a walk outside with the dog, or a coffee break in the lounge chair—whatever guilty pleasure you want. But you only get to do it if you have done the exercises in your time block.

In addition to setting up a reward system for yourself to stay on track, researchers also suggest setting up reminders of your goals as a way keep your eye on the prize and focus on the big picture. You decide what type of reminder works best for you. Some of my coaching clients have written their goals on sticky notes and placed them on their monitors. Others use a visual reminder of their goal, like a place they want to visit, a home update they want to do, or a photo of a loved one they provide for. A few recall a feeling they had when they once overcame or accomplished something.

Rather than trying to fight our present bias, use it, harness it. When you see, hear, or feel your goal reminder, that is your cue to think about how the present task will lead to the future goal. It is almost as if we need to keep the vision of the future state around us—much like the person who puts the skinny picture of themselves on the fridge to see a vision of themselves after they reach their goal, and to remind themselves that their current actions will get them there.

Perfectionism Bias

I put off writing this book for far too many years. I would start, feel as if it was not good enough, and then stop. Then I would be inspired to start again, do it for a bit, and stop again because it still wasn't good enough. This cycle continued for about five years.

Perfectionism is a symptom of an out-of-control need for approval.

I knew I had high standards and expectations for myself, and I told myself that these expectations are what helped me become successful. The reality was that I was letting my own need for approval take over.

When is perfectionism bad for us, and when is it good? When your first reaction is to find fault and be overly critical of mistakes, it's bad. If you procrastinate taking action on a project out of fear of failure, it's bad. It doesn't help you when you dismiss compliments and don't celebrate your success because you think it wasn't good enough, or you think the people who are saying these things are just trying to be nice. When perfectionism leads to procrastination, we avoid challenges, buy into rigid all-or-nothing thinking, make toxic comparisons (thank you, social media), and adopt a closed mindset that shuts down our creativity. It makes our world small and dark.

This fear of failure, this feeling of unworthiness and low self-esteem, can come from adverse childhood experiences and may contribute to depression, anxiety, obsessive-compulsive disorders, and suicidal thoughts. Which is again why consistent mental health practices—and a good therapist—are so important.

The easiest way to put off prospecting is to obsess over the perfect pitch, manuscript, message, or voicemail. I was always able to come up with all sorts of reasons why I couldn't reach out to people yet. Maybe you will recognize a few:

- My offering isn't ready!
- They don't look like the right person to reach out to.
- They're busy and won't have the time or patience for me.
- It's going to take too long to reach out to each of these people individually—maybe I should send an email to everyone.

- The subject line needs to grab their attention. I better work on that and research what works best.
- This email is too long (too short, has too many exclamation points…).
- If they need me, they'll reach out to me.

In addition to earlier strategies I described, like reducing social media time and being more kind in the way you talk to yourself, you can also try one or more of these daily habits to overcome a need for approval:

1. **Slow it all down.** Like me, you might think that meditating is one of those things you don't have time for. How does sitting around and breathing help you get things done? No one ever accomplished anything by sitting around! It wasn't until I started practicing mindfulness, yoga, and meditation that I started to see that it isn't about achieving perfection as some future state, but seeing and accepting the perfection of the moment I am in. The breathing techniques physically slow down your heart rate, helping you to relax and be in the present moment. This allows you to actively listen when talking with your buyers.

2. **Give yourself deadlines.** I know, it seems counterintuitive to the previous point, but you must have a stopping point. You can't keep obsessing over the details for all eternity. Your message, timing, and delivery may never be perfect, but it can be good enough to try, and then allow it to evolve from there. By giving yourself a deadline, you open your mindset to the idea that everything is an experiment. You become more able to keep your perfectionism in check, and you feed a growth mindset too. Setting a deadline with my publisher,

for example, was the best thing I did for myself during this process—otherwise I would still be obsessing over this chapter. A deadline that you set with someone else is a commitment device that you can use to limit how much time you spend worrying over the details.

3 **Play outside your box.** This one comes straight from my therapist, who told me to read Brené Brown's research on perfectionism. When you are a child at play, you aren't worried about getting it exactly right, or about what other people think; you are living in your own little world and playing to your own tune. As adults, when we step outside our usual boxes and play imperfectly, it opens our minds to our inner child again, the one who had fun and didn't care what others thought. For me, it was taking horseback riding lessons. I hadn't been around horses in over twenty years, but when one of my sons started, I joined him. As I flopped around on a horse for the first few times, laughing the whole way, I didn't have time to worry about how I looked, or how well I was doing. I was putting all my focus on trying to figure out how to stand and post at a trot without falling off.

Do not expect to eliminate your perfectionism and procrastination. That would only feed it. Instead, expect and accept that there will be times that it happens. When it does, be brave, dig deep, and don't hide from your task. Brave people struggle too, but they don't hide from that struggle—they take it head-on. You can either be too strong to fail, or too scared to try. The choice is always yours.

When you do the research on your buyers, it will be easier to know what to say. Start with the people closest to you to get context on the insights you find through research. But don't stop there—develop small daily practices to overcome the fear of rejection and those perfectionist tendencies that lead to inaction. Set a date for yourself of when you will create a list of people to reach out to for "interviews." Use the sample email script from earlier in this chapter to reach out and schedule conversations, adapting it as you need for LinkedIn or phone calls. Remember, this isn't about you—it's about finding those who need help.

Time to Get Going!

If you have been following the exercises so far, then you are ready. It's time for you to start selling with others. Start with your initial list of suspects and referrers. The rest of the chapters in this book will guide you into having your first conversations with buyers, people whom you suspect might have a problem that you can solve.

What will you commit to? How many will you reach out to today? Start with one. One is one more than you did yesterday. The next day, reach out to two, then three. Build your prospecting muscle as if it were an exercise habit that you up the level on every day.

Write your commitment down, then share it with someone.

I will call on:

____

By this day/time:

____

KEY ACTIONS AND TAKEAWAYS

You do not have to cold-call strangers to prospect (but don't rule it out!). Do your research and immerse yourself in your buyer's world to understand how they define and understand their problem, then start your prospecting among the people you know. Treat prospecting like an interview in which you are trying to learn, not pitch.

Know that it won't go perfectly, and create a reward system for yourself to overcome the natural tendency to procrastinate.

6

UNCOVER YOUR MVPS

If you want something done right, do it yourself.

MY MOM

SHORTLY AFTER I started my sales consultancy, a mentor convinced me and a strategic partner that we should create an online course that we could enroll large numbers of people into.

We spent a few hours crunching the numbers on a spreadsheet to see how many people we could put through the course and the price we would charge. As the numbers in Excel got higher and higher, so did my excitement.

We figured that with a twelve-week course, if we could get a hundred people to sign up for it, at $1,000 apiece, we could cash in $100,000 a quarter. Naturally, some of the people who took the course would want more one-on-one coaching, and so for every 1 percent (or ten people) we converted, we would gain an additional $60,000 without having to try. It would be repeatable business because it was all online. I would be sipping piña coladas on the beach and still making money!

That idea sent me into a flurry of activity. For weeks I did nothing else other than make cold calls, blast emails to everyone on my lists, and post endlessly on social media. When I wasn't blasting the course out to everyone with a pulse or Twitter account, I was locked in my office with my PowerPoint, putting together the slides that would make us rich.

After eight weeks of constant promotion and innumerable PowerPoint edits, we were ready for the students and cash to come flooding in.

One person signed up.

One!

I couldn't believe it. What was the point? What a waste of time and resources that I would never get back.

That failure sidelined my confidence in my ability to succeed in this new venture and version of my business. Not only that, it also damaged the strategic partnerships involved, and I took a hit to my reputation.

How do all those people who advertise their courses and claim to be making all this money do it? I didn't know what we had done wrong, which meant that I didn't know how to make it better. So I put the idea aside.

I wish I could say that I learned my lesson the first time this happened. But I did not, and they were expensive lessons. What I came to learn as I tried and failed to launch new products and services was that one thing was missing from all my planning and promotion.

My buyer.

The person who all this was for. I had planned a party for them, never asking what party they wanted, and then I was surprised that they weren't interested in my invite.

"Build it, then sell it" is a common misconception. Maybe you have made this same mistake yourself, or you don't want to believe that you have, so you lock yourself away to create your products and services, detailing out every possible scenario, maybe hiring people to help you... only to find that after weeks, months, and years of thinking, planning, and building, very few people are interested or willing to pay for what you've so painstakingly invented.

Maybe it's the marketing? Yes, more marketing—that's what you need (insert sarcasm here).

How many times have you gone down that path, given up, and had to start all over again?

My mom was wrong. The only way to do something right is to collaborate, not to do it yourself.

The beauty of collaboration with your buyer is that it answers your most pressing questions about what the Most Valuable Problems your buyer has, what your Most Valuable Products will be, and what the Most Valuable Process is to sell with your buyer.

This is MVP to the third power.

And if you have already created your offering, or you work in a company that has—you still can (and should) collaborate with your buyers.

Collaboration isn't only about the offering, the sales process, and/or the skills you have. Your buyers are the sun, and everything you do in your business is the planets and moons that revolve around it. This means that collaboration with your buyers can't be your sales process alone, it also has to be in the creation of your products and services.

The Value of Collaboration

After that failed online course, I participated in Danny Iny's Course Builder's Laboratory and learned that the reason so many online courses and services fail is that the sellers are not collaborating with their buyers on the product they want and need. They don't place value on the solution you offer. This is due to what researchers Michael Irwin Norton, Daniel Mochon, and Dan Ariely call the IKEA Effect: we like—and value—things more if we've expended effort to create them. This same effect applies to something that was made for you by someone like you.

I had locked myself away in an ivory tower to design a masterpiece that I would bestow onto my subjects, and they rejected it. I made the mistake most business owners make—I followed my passion first, which caused me to leave out the most important part: who I was solving a problem for. As sellers, we falsely believe that our idea will sell itself or that there's no point in visiting a prospective customer without a finished product in hand.

In a study of 120 entrepreneurs published in *Harvard Business Review*, Vincent Onyemah, Martha Rivera Pesquera, and Abdul Ali found that more than half of the participants had created their offering before getting feedback from buyers—and felt that it was a big mistake. They didn't spend enough time listening to their prospects' reactions. As a result, they tried discounts to close initial deals, relied on early sales to family and friends, and did not choose their first customers and clients strategically.

The study also found that when those entrepreneurs did go on sales calls, many had to face tough questions about whether their offering would work, if they were credible and had the right experience, the size of their companies, their prices, and the cost of switching to an unproven offering.

After my many failed attempts to launch a virtual course, I took these lessons and ran an experiment to build a six-week virtual course pilot. Following the steps from the Course Builder's Laboratory, I researched what was out there, conducted interviews to learn from my ideal students, came up with a course outline, and shared what I had built based on their feedback.

With this process, I was able to get ten paying students in my first pilot course. I was pleasantly surprised, not only by the initial success, but also by the unexpected results and lessons that my pilot students taught me.

First, I learned that after intensive one-to-one coaching and training with me, previous clients wanted a way to keep learning, but didn't need those intense daily interactions. I had thought that the course would be a stepping stone for new students, not a reinforcement for previous ones.

Second, I discovered that my clients and students wanted a community, a place where they could safely share their own challenges and experiences outside of their workplaces. Selling as a full-time profession can be isolating—especially if you are working remotely—as is being a business owner, so knowing that others struggle with some of the same things we do can help us overcome those struggles.

Third, I didn't expect that the most basic first steps of goal setting and motivation (coming up in chapters 9 and 10) would be the most transformative thing for my students and clients.

Finally, I was encouraged when my pilot students were eager to keep learning and wanted to sit in on future classes, going so far as to recommend and refer the course to other students.

I had planned to do the pilot course one time, and then take the feedback to finalize the online on-demand course. What ended up happening is that, for the next eighteen months, I had dozens of new students go through my pilot course. It eventually got the attention of a large company, who asked me to do the course for a team that was transitioning into a more traditional sales role.

The one thing that made all this happen was that I collaborated with my first group of students. Because of that collaboration, those students placed more value on it, which led to them telling their peers about it—and so those peers placed more value on it as well.

What might happen if you do the same for your new and current products and services?

And if you are selling an existing product or offering that you do not have the ability to alter or change, how could you apply this principle to how you sell it with your buyers?

Interview the People around You

This may seem like a very old-fashioned way to prospect, but it can save you hours, if not days and weeks, of scrolling through the internet, not to mention thousands of dollars on online advertising. When you talk to people who are in the role of your ideal buyer, or who talk with those people on a regular basis, you can get firsthand context on what you found during your initial research.

Who can you talk to? If you have done the exercises in the previous chapter to find your people, you have an idea. I recommend that you start with the list of people you know personally who are similar to the person who could be your buyer. For example, if you are selling a product or solution for other small business owners, call your aunt or cousin who owns a business, or entrepreneur friends that you grew up with or went to school with. Perhaps you offer consulting to manufacturing companies and have a friend of the family who is a general manager at one. Or you sell marketing software to ad agencies and have a neighbor who works for a local agency. In my own business, I train companies on how to hire salespeople, and so I find myself working with a lot of HR professionals. Turns out, my neighbor was in HR for forty years and was more than happy to help me understand this new buyer. Even though I had built out the program, my research and initial conversations helped me to understand what the most important aspects would be and the best ways to customize my messaging accordingly.

You know people. You simply might not realize it.

Okay, but what if you think you really *don't* know people? Maybe you are going into a totally new industry and don't know anyone personally who could help fill you in on the missing details. That's okay—this is what your list of referrals is for. That list includes those people who know or work with your buyers. Who do you know who works with your buyers in some other way?

By now, you have done the work to research your buyer's world, and you have reached out to ask for a time to talk. Now, what do you say to them? What is the best way to engage with them? How should the conversation go?

The Buyer First Rules of Engagement

Remember the experience I had with my doctors after my thyroid cancer diagnosis? Maybe you have had similar experiences with your own health when you've gone to the doctor for an issue. They ask a few questions, say it's nothing, write you a prescription, and send you on your way.

How likely are you to trust that doctor and follow their advice?

What if, instead, you went to your doctor and asked why you are having symptoms. The doctor asks a question, you answer, then they ask more questions about your answer. You go back and forth, digging into possible scenarios and options for each. Finally, the doctor asks, "You know your body better than anyone. What do you think about this option versus this one? Which is more doable?" Together you come up with more questions that need answers, along with a plan to address them.

Now how likely are you to trust that doctor and follow their advice?

This is how a buyer first conversation should sound.

Whether you are a business owner trying to find your first (or next) customer or a seller in a company, there are some basic rules of engagement you should follow when talking with your buyers.

In fact, these rules apply to almost all conversations—in sales, with your kids, or with your friends, loved ones, and larger family.

And when you are looking for places and people to practice with, those closest to you are the easiest ones to start with.

Rule Number 1: Make It #notaboutme

Say it out loud, over and over and over again: "It's not about me." The intent of listening, language, and questions should be one of other-focused curiosity. To do this, you need to be fully present, actively listening, and asking enough good questions.

I am sure you have had the experience—or know someone who has—of *that* person. You know that person. The one who only talks about themselves: what they are doing, and what they think about anything and everything. The one who never stops to ask about you. The one who interrupts you in your story to tell you how the same thing happened to them. I've been that person before. You may have too. Talking about ourselves and what we want will not be tolerated for long by our buyers. But it is so easy to do! Why is that?

In a 2012 study from Harvard University, neurologists Diana Tamir and Jason Mitchell used functional MRI technology to study people's brains as they held conversations. When participants were asked to state their own opinions on something, it "increased activity in the area of the brain associated with reward and pleasure." Our brains crave reward—it is natural to want to talk about ourselves. It also means that our buyers enjoy answering these types of questions! Now that you know this, you know that the win for you is that your buyer is open to sharing what they think.

Not only do "clarification and elaboration" questions appeal to buyers, they also help us as sellers to understand our buyers better. A Stanford University study by Frances Chen, Julia Minson, and Zakary Tormala showed that when people ask elaboration questions, it helps them understand others' viewpoints (so, you as the seller would understand your buyer better). Beyond that, the study found that these types of questions help the person being asked be more receptive to other ideas, even if they are contrary to their own (so, your buyer would be more receptive to your ideas).

This is how we build trust.

When we ask buyer first questions, it helps us understand our buyers better and helps our buyers see the value in making a change. Selling with our buyers comes from the mastery of the art and science of asking enough thought-provoking questions to challenge our buyers' thinking, and offering insights that help them understand the new options. Our ability to do that depends on how well we can stay in the moment and keep our need for approval in check.

This is why our own mental game is so critical to being buyer first and successful in our sales roles. If you skipped chapter 4—"Get Your Head in the Game"—go back!

Rule Number 2: Create Custom Questions and Content

In LinkedIn's 2020 *State of Sales Report*, a survey of executive decision makers suggests that 90 percent of executives ignore irrelevant and impersonal messages. Seems low, doesn't it? (I would have thought it closer to 100 percent! Who are the 10 percent of executives who pay attention to spam?) Research is the foundation for personalization, because it gives us the clues to personalize our messaging and questions with content that is relevant to our audience. Remember the sales leader in chapter 5 whom BDR Charlie researched prior to reaching out to him? A little time spent pays off big.

Say it out loud,
over and over
and over again:
“It’s not about me.”

This doesn't mean you have to write a brand-new message for everyone, but you should be able to add in the personal details that make a message unique to them. This is why you do your research first—so you know what to customize with.

In a behavioral study designed for B2B DecisionLabs by Zakary Tormala—one of the Stanford researchers from that "clarification and elaboration" study—305 individuals were tested to see how questions impact the persuasion of a message. The research team found that you can "enhance the persuasive power of a message by sharing an insight before posing diagnostic questions."

This study reflects the well-known Anchoring Effect, which is a cognitive bias that describes our tendency to rely on the first piece of information offered (the "anchor") when making decisions. We use that initial piece of information to make subsequent judgments. You can often see this effect at play in pricing conversations, when you hear things like: "Normally the cost is $10,000, but for you we are offering it at $8,000." We hear $10,000 first, and so our decision to buy at $8,000 is based on that.

Do you see now why the research in the previous chapter is critical to creating the questions and messaging that will resonate with your buyers?

Rule Number 3: Quantify the Impact

If you can't quantify the impact of a problem, is it real? Not to most buyers, it isn't. Abstract ROI calculations by themselves do not do enough here—in fact, they can be counterproductive, thanks to what psychologists call "preference stability." When we have a problem, challenge, or question, we quickly form our own opinion on how best to solve it, and we do not want to change our minds once they are made up. In fact, we will ignore or discount information that doesn't align with what we have already decided. This helps explain how some people hold fast to a belief despite a mountain of evidence that proves otherwise. You've seen this happen firsthand when you've heard two people debating over a political issue, or the color of a dress.

When we offer up known information to a buyer ("it looks as if you are trying to do XYZ...") we are merely reinforcing that preference stability. Your buyer is unlikely to pay attention to the message because it isn't anything that they don't know—in their minds, what they have already figured out is good enough. Instead of the same old information, offer a quantifiable business impact of the problem, one that they don't know about or haven't fully considered. This can make them think, "Maybe I should check this out—what if there is something I don't know about here?" It leads them to realize that they don't know what they don't know: "Maybe what I am thinking isn't good enough after all."

Some of my coaching clients sell CRM technology, and one of the things these sellers look for is companies that are hiring salespeople. Before coaching, their messaging to these companies all sounded the same. It was all about them as the seller, and it lacked quantifiable information that had an emotional appeal. "Looks like you are hiring a lot of salespeople, which usually means you are trying to scale growth—our all-in-one CRM solution is easy to use so you can track your growth..."

An approach that applies quantified impact would look something like this: "We have found through conversations with some of your competitors who are hiring salespeople that they are overestimating their return on sales hire (ROSH) due to longer onboarding and ramp-up times because it takes longer for a new salesperson to be productive due to inefficient and outdated systems. Many executives are frustrated with how long it takes IT to revamp those systems, so the projects often get pushed off or delayed—leaving new sellers to figure out a system on their own. That means as much as 15 percent of revenue is lost between the time a new seller starts and when they are productive."

Rule Number 4: Use Emotional Descriptors

The use of specific emotional words and language is how our brains recall memories. The more detail we use, the easier it is for others to create a visual representation of what we are talking about.

The year I turned eighteen, I decided to stay up all night on New Year's Eve so I could see the sunrise the next day. When an ice storm prevented me from going out that night, I decided to take a walk in the woods at dawn instead. The air was crisp and sharp, but the sun's rays warmed my face as my feet smashed through the ice-crusted snow. As I reached the ridge next to the river behind my house, the ice on the trees was starting to crack from the heat—the sound of breaking glass echoed through the woods. I looked up and saw tiny rainbows surrounding me as the sun reflected through the ice.

I will never forget that New Year's Day. And now you have a vivid sense of it too.

Think about your favorite memories. You may recall a smell, an image, a sound—the more details you remember, the more real the memory is to you. Now think about what happens when you share that memory with others who were there with you, and how they add their details (and corresponding emotional ties) to it.

Specifics are memorable because they mobilize the brain, according to Carmen Simon, a cognitive neuroscientist at B2B DecisionLabs. When you carefully choose what Simon calls the "telling details," you attract more attention and ignite people's senses, which leads to stronger and more precise memories.

We know from science that we make decisions almost instantly in the emotional, intuitive part of our brain that responds to new information and avoids risk. Sometimes we don't know that we have made the decision yet. But, once we do, the rational, analytical part of our brain takes over to justify the decision. While ROI and quantitative impact doesn't drive our decision, it is still a tool we use to explain our decisions to ourselves and to others.

Emotion first, logic second.

Rule Number 5: Compare and Contrast

For our buyers to make a change—and change is exactly what you are selling—there needs to be a big enough gap between where they are and where they want to be, otherwise known as cognitive dissonance. When we talk in chapter 9 about setting your own goals for change, you'll learn that the gap between your current state and your future state must be wide enough and compelling enough to drive you to make a change. If it isn't a big enough difference, then why would you go through the work, effort, and risk of change only to see similar results as before? You won't, and don't. It's a waste of time. It is true for you and for your buyers.

By creating a verbal picture of the contrast between the current and future states, you will help your buyers to act.

Preparing for Your Conversation

How might these rules of engagement play out in your initial outreach to your buyers? First, let's look at how you can use them to prepare for those conversations.

When you think of your first conversation (or first part of the conversation) as an interview, it can take some of the pressure off. You are here not to pitch, convince, or persuade. Only to ask, listen, and understand.

Make sure to send your buyer a calendar invite with the call-in details as soon as they agree to talk with you. If you are meeting in person, include the location of where you will meet. To make sure that you can stay fully present in the conversation and not get wrapped up in taking excessive notes, ask your buyer if they will be comfortable with you using the Zoom recording function, your iPhone, or an app like Otter.ai to record the conversation so you can refer to it later.

A day or two prior to your scheduled conversation, send a reminder email, text message, or social media direct message to confirm the day, time, and length of the meeting. Remind them of what you are talking about, thank them for talking to you about the topic, let them know you will have some prepared questions, and give them three examples of those questions to get them thinking. Ask if they have questions too, or if there are specific things they would like to learn about in the time you have together. Remember: this is a collaboration—always and in all ways.

When you start off the conversation, build some rapport by asking a few questions about them. If could be about something they recently posted on social, or about something in the background on their Zoom window. Be curious about their education and how it led them to where they are now. Yes, asking about the weather and sports is okay—if that is what your buyer is into. (Personally, I love to talk about the weather in different places because I love the outdoors and I like to travel.) This is where all that research you did to inform yourself on what to talk about will help you. My own goal in rapport building is to try to get someone to smile and laugh a little. This puts people in a good mood—laughter releases those feel-good hormones—and studies suggest that when we are in a good frame of mind, we are more open minded and willing to trust.

Does this happen all the time? No.

Ellie retired from the military in Israel and became an enterprise sales rep for a large tech company. She knew how to work hard and get things done. But in her new role she was frustrated that, while she was getting plenty of opportunities to talk with people, those conversations didn't seem to go anywhere. She was about to fly to Europe to attend an event that one of her top potential buyers would be at. We had been working on her sales mindsets and skills for a few weeks, and had brainstormed and practiced the conversation repeatedly.

Ellie and her buyer arranged a day and time to meet, and drafted an agenda. However, at the meeting, he met all of her attempts to build rapport with one-word answers. Before coaching, she told me, she would have plowed through and stuck to the agenda, not noticing that he was checked out. This time, she was able to realize that he wasn't his usual self—he had seemed warm and responsive on the phone a few days ago. Rather than ignore it and keep forging ahead, she stopped and asked him, "How are you feeling today?"

Surprised by her question, he blurted out, "Awful. My flight was delayed twice, and my wife is texting me about an issue with our son. Now I've found out my presentation got moved to earlier and I am exhausted."

"Then you must be totally excited to talk about chat bots with me!" she said. He chuckled and shook his head.

Ellie stopped the meeting right there and suggested they move to another time. He smiled at her in gratitude. She later told me that they texted back and forth over the next few days to share parenting and travel tips. When they had their rescheduled meeting, he told her, "You won me over with your human approach."

Do not underestimate the power of rapport, small talk, and being fully present—especially if you can make someone laugh.

In a 2017 study published in the journal *Industrial Marketing Management*, Bruno Lussier and his research team surveyed

149 salesperson-customer relationships across multiple industries. The results suggested that a salesperson's use of humor positively influences their creativity and customer trust. In addition, customer trust influences word-of-mouth and the expectation of a continued relationship.

How does using humor build trust?

Think about what happens when you really laugh: you throw your head back, you expose your neck—you make yourself vulnerable. We laugh with people we trust.

Laughter also releases oxytocin, which is often called the "love hormone" or the "bonding molecule." Paul J. Zak in the *Wall Street Journal* called it the "trust molecule," referencing extensive research into oxytocin as a social behavior moderator and its significant implications in business and global commerce.

This applies whenever we're thinking about how we position our opening statements to people on the phone, or how we handle customer issues. When we use humor it helps build trust, and it reduces stress for customers who are having issues.

But trust is not built on laughter alone. Your buyer needs to feel that you understand them and their world. The research you did in chapter 5 will serve you well, because it has likely helped you uncover an insight to share with them and ask more about.

Brainstorming Your Questions

Once you have found a connection and set your first meeting with your buyer, it's time to think about the questions to ask them in the "interview."

You know these questions already—they are the whos, whats, wheres, whens, whys, and hows. This is about more than what questions *you* want answers to—it's about what questions *they* want answers to. What do you need to learn about your buyers?

What do they need to know about you? The answers you get will help inform you on what capabilities are most important to them, how they make their decisions, and what is at stake for them.

To help you brainstorm questions, open the "**Buyer First Questions Framework**" from the **Buyer First Workbook**, which you can download from **bit.ly/buyerfirstworkbook.** Remember the Number 1 Buyer First Rule of Engagement: make it #notaboutme. Check yourself: are your questions as much about what your buyers care about as they are about what you need to sell them?

Think of the worksheets you have downloaded as a road map to align your questions to your buyer's decision-making process. With that process in mind, you can effectively brainstorm the questions to ask in your calls.

Not every question in the framework is going to be relevant to you and your buyer. Instead, customize it with the most important and relevant questions according to who your buyer is and where you think they are in their decision-making process.

I am often asked if there is such a thing as asking too many questions. In an article from the AI call recording company Gong, Chris Orlob suggests that the analysis of thousands of sales calls indicates that the most successful sales conversations have eleven to fourteen questions per conversation—or, for conversations with a C-level executive, between six and eight.

Your questions will happen in phases, but not always in a linear fashion—which can seem hard to organize and keep on track. Writing the questions down until they become second nature will help you learn to move through them in a natural conversation with your buyers. For each phase of questions, you can align the stage of your buyer's process and your corresponding sales process.

Your first phase of questions should help you understand what is happening with them right now. This part of the sales process is commonly called the initial discovery phase. In truth, this phase never ends, because things will change with your buyers. A consistent practice of uncovering unmet needs and goals is how you keep any good relationship moving forward. While Gartner's 2020 *Future of B2B Buying* research suggests that 33 percent of all buyers prefer digital channels to talking with sales (and that goes up to 44 percent among millennial buyers), there is a point when they'll want to talk. (Gartner's research suggests that those who don't talk to a salesperson have a 23 percent higher purchase regret. Buyers still need sellers.)

When they do talk to you, you don't know what they know, and they don't know what you know. Create the questions that bridge this gap and that put you both on the same place on the map. What is the situation they are in? What do they think the problem is? What do they think about it? How is everyone around them acting? Ultimately, you want to learn what their status quo is, how it came to be, and what they have tried before.

What follows is a list of questions to get you started in each phase of your early conversations with suspected buyers.

Phase 1 Questions: Uncover the Current Status Quo

At this first stage, your buyer has likely educated themselves and explored what options are available to them. Your goal is to understand the problem as your buyer sees it and determine if it is something you can help with. You want to understand how they frame the problem in their mind and how they're going about looking for solutions. This is also your opportunity to uncover where they are in their buying process. Perhaps they are still trying to figure out what the problem is, or maybe they know and are trying to understand if it is something they need to fix now, and, if so, what options they have. Here is your first phase of questions to ask:

- **How did they find you?** If it was a referral, how do they know the person who referred you? What had they been talking about when your name came up? If you found them through your own outreach, what piqued their curiosity when you reached out to them? Or if they found you through a web search or filled something out on your website, what were they looking for? What else did their searches turn up?

- **Why were they looking?** What is going on and how would they describe their current situation? How did they become aware of it? (Was it something they observed, heard, or were told to do?) Who is responsible for it? What have they tried? What made them go in that direction to handle it? How long has it been this way? What makes this such a challenge for them? What do they believe causes the problem?

After this initial phase of sample questions, summarize what you've heard so far. If you know of a data point from your research that would be relevant to what they said, share that information and follow it up with an insight on how it might impact them. Then ask a diagnostic question to move into the next phase, where you can learn about why this is a problem for them and what they believe a solution should be.

In my own work, when I'm talking with business owners, sales leaders, and human resource professionals about trying to hire salespeople, I have learned from them that while they did know everyone was struggling to recruit sales candidates, they didn't know that some were seeing lower attrition rates and higher rates of success because of their hiring process. Many tried recruiters and ads to find people—strategies they have always used—but it was getting more expensive and only had a 50 percent success rate. They weren't sure what to do differently, only that they needed to do something.

Unfortunately, this is where most business owners and sellers stop asking. They have "discovered" the pain point or challenge to pitch their solution to. But the reason so many buyers stop responding or become indecisive, causing opportunities to delay, is because no one has dug deeper to uncover, clarify, and elaborate why this is a problem at all.

Which brings us to our next phase of questions. After getting a level of understanding about what your suspected buyer's problem (or opportunity) is, the next phase is to understand why they believe it is a problem.

Phase 2 Questions: Dig Into Why It Is a Problem

This thread of questions needs to explore deeper into what you discovered in the first phase by asking potential buyers to give their perspectives and explain more about what they stated in the first layer of answers.

Why is this so important? Remember the study by Chen, Minson, and Tormala that showed how "elaboration questions" help the asker understand the viewpoints of the other person—meaning they can help sellers empathize with buyers? The same study found that these types of questions help the person being asked (the buyer) be more receptive to other ideas—including ideas that are contrary to their own. Surveys and studies all point to the fact that buyers want sellers to help them think differently about their problem. And don't forget the Harvard University study by Tamir and Mitchell showing that people enjoy answering these types of questions!

Here are some examples of the second phase of questions. You can find more of these in the Phase 2 section of the "**Buyer First Questions Framework**" in the package you have downloaded.

- **Who or what else does this problem impact?** Who is affected by this? What is their perspective on it?
- **What do they believe about the problem?** Why did you decide to go in this direction to solve the problem? Why not continue to do it that way? What other options are you considering? What do you think the best solution is? Why do you think previous solutions didn't work?
- **What obstacles are preventing change or success?** Are there company policies that stand in the way? Do certain people think there is a different way to solve the problem? What about the process itself is difficult to change?

When I dug deeper with my own buyers to understand the impact of not being able to hire good-fit salespeople, I learned that, for business owners, it affected their ability to work with their boards and investors, who didn't trust the sales forecasts because they had been missed so many times in the past. For sales leaders, the impact was on the morale of their teams, and the ability they had to motivate those teams to do what needed to be done. And for HR professionals, they were bearing the brunt of everyone's frustrations because it took so long to get someone in, only to have them leave. Everyone wanted a proven and repeatable process for hiring, but no one could seem to agree on the right way to do it.

Whether you are starting from zero or have been at this for a few years and have your own list of contacts, when you ask people what their frustrations and fears are, what they have tried and what has and hasn't worked, and what they think the reasons for that are, you have started to collaborate with them.

Phase 3 Questions: Qualify on Why It Is Important to Fix

The third phase of questions is perhaps my favorite because it gets to why this is important to fix. What are the consequences if it is not fixed? How will it impact them? This gets to the buying motivation, or the reason to change the status quo. It also gets buyers to move closer to what they desire or wish to avoid. Understanding how they think they will benefit from the solution enables you to show how your solution satisfies that buying motive. This is another way you can build trust with buyers: they will feel that you "get" them. This phase of questions gets to the buyer's commitment to change. Without a compelling reason to change and a gap large enough between where they are and where they want to be, it will be difficult to help them take action.

Here are a few examples of qualification questions to determine their commitment to make a decision and a change:

- **What is the cost of not fixing the issue?** Will they get more complaints from those impacted? Will they incur unnecessary costs? Will they lose to their competitors? How will profits be affected?
- **When do they need results by?** Is there an impending event? What results do they need to see before then? When does the cost of the problem become too great? What is the timeline to implement the solution and use it? How does that timeline align with when they need to see results by?
- **What happens to them when they see the results they need?** Will it mean a promotion for them? More income, respect, or recognition?

When I ask these questions of my own buyers, this is when I find out whether I can help them—and whether they truly want help. If they do want help, these questions will uncover why. For my own buyers, I would hear answers related to revenue, investment, or having to let people go. One business leader told me that they could disrupt an entire industry and secure their legacy—but only if they could solve this issue.

Phase 4 Questions: Build Out the Decision Requirements

Once you have learned what the current status quo is, why it is a problem, and why it is important to them to fix it, you can start to collaborate with them on what a possible solution would look like and how the decision will get made. This is most likely where you will need to draw a quantifiable impact and use emotional descriptors to describe a solution.

- **How will this solution help?** Summarize the business problem with detailed emotional language, the capabilities you have to solve the problem, and the value of those capabilities. What do they believe the impact would be?
- **Who else needs to be involved?** Do they make the decision alone, or do they need input or approval from others? What do those who are impacted need to know? What is important to them? How do they want to get involved? When in the process do they need to be involved?
- **How does the decision get made?** What information do they need to make a decision? What are the steps they need to go through internally? How long does that process typically take?

Remember that all the questions in each of these phases are meant to be customized according to what you have learned in your research about your buyer and through using the Buyer First Rules of Engagement. Once you have written out your questions, practice saying them out loud to yourself. If there are parts that you stumble over, or that don't sound natural to you, rewrite them and say them out loud again until it feels more natural.

Throughout the question asking process, pause and reflect with your buyer. Do not merely run through these lists verbatim, but instead use them as a guide for planning and practicing what to ask. At regular intervals, summarize what you have heard and ask your buyer if there is anything more you should know or that they want to add or change, then move on to the next topic or phase of questions. Make note of the things that you heard that surprised you and ask more about those areas.

Once you feel at ease saying your questions out loud, raise the stakes and bring a partner into your practice. Ask your family, friends, or neighbors to practice the conversation with you. The more you step outside of your comfort zone, the more improvement you will see in your skills and mindsets.

Keep in mind that not every single question given here needs to be asked. Remember the data from Gong: most successful sales calls don't have more than fourteen questions.

Out in the Wild

Using my own business as an example, I often speak to business leaders in startups and growing corporations about how best to hire salespeople to more predictably grow revenue. Our industry has barely broken a 50 percent success rate, and while how we train and coach sellers has a large impact on that success rate, it often starts with who was hired for what role, and how they were hired. Most do not have the right people in the right roles that are best suited for them—a recipe for employee churn and internal culture clashes.

Here is how a recent conversation went with the president of a technology company who had heard me during an online interview. I used the Buyer First Questions Framework. Pay particular attention to the bolded questions and the overall flow.

Phase 1 Questions: Uncover the Current Status Quo

"Hi John," I said. "Thank you for your kind words after listening to my interview. You mentioned that you wanted to learn more about the hiring process I teach—**what did I say during the interview that piqued your interest?"**

"You had me at data from over two million salespeople and a 91 percent overall success rate. Is that for real?" John asked.

"I know," I said. "It can seem hard to believe when traditionally you are lucky if you have a 50 percent success rate. But when companies use our data to guide hiring decisions, and optimize the hiring process to be more objective and standardized, those results are for real—because hiring salespeople is unlike any other role you will hire for in your company. **What is happening now in your sales teams?"**

John described how hardly any of his salespeople were doing enough outreach or proper follow-up. He noted that he had just got off the phone with one of his sellers, who couldn't tell him what the next steps were on most of their opportunities. I asked him, **"What have you already tried to correct the problem?"** John explained that they had done training on a popular enterprise sales process that he had used at his previous company, but no one was doing it consistently.

He finished with, "As you said in your interview, when you have the wrong people in the wrong roles, no amount of training or coaching is going to make a square peg fit into a round hole."

Phase 2 Questions: Dig Into Why It Is a Problem

At this point, I summarized with John what I had heard so far and shared with him that not only did issues with poor-fit hires hurt current revenue attainment (not to mention morale and culture), a failed sales hire can also cost a company the equivalent of a round of funding due to the time it takes to hire, onboard, and train new salespeople, plus the cost of lost future revenue. Knowing that they had recently received funding to go after a new market from a private equity firm, I asked what his investment board thought about the problem—in other words, **"Who else does this problem impact?"**

That really got him fired up. He told me they had spent a quarter of a million dollars in recruiting fees alone so far that year for hires who were not working out six months later—and the investment board was not thrilled. They believed that the company needed to start over again and hire all new salespeople.

"If recruiters are not giving you the quality candidates you need, what other options are you considering?" I asked.

John shared that he believed they could do a better job with an internal recruiter, and he had a leader on his team with recruiting experience.

"What obstacles do you foresee with that option?"

"I don't see how he is going to have time," he replied. "We need to hire twenty people in the next three months, and it is taking him ten to fifteen hours to sort through resumes and do the interviews. It isn't scalable. He still has other responsibilities to manage a team and assist on strategic work with marketing. We have a human resources team, but they don't have sales experience to really know what to look for."

I nodded and said, "I can see how that is putting you between a rock and hard place: no one has the time to do the recruiting internally given the current process, and external recruiters are expensive—and more so when their contracts only guarantee the first six months. If your sales cycle is longer than that, it's too late to know if they are going to work out. That is why optimizing the hiring process is as important as using objective data that is specific to the role. When you objectively identify what they will need to succeed, you can screen candidates and only spend time on the resumes and interviews for the best fits. In fact, by implementing the standardized process we teach, hiring teams cut their hiring times from an average of ten to fifteen hours per hire to four hours, which allows your leaders to focus on other revenue generating activities."

Phase 3 Questions: Qualify on Why It Is Important to Fix

"John, you mentioned that you need to hire twenty salespeople in the next three months," I went on to say. "**What revenue targets do you need them to reach, and by when?**"

John shared the information, and I asked, "**What is important about that number and that timeframe?**" He answered that they were milestones they had to meet in order to get the next round of funding to further develop the technology. (He saw this question coming—he is in sales, after all.) At this point, we had some good rapport (we had bonded over growing up in the country and all the quirks that come with it), so I felt comfortable asking him a personal question.

"**When you hire the right salespeople, hit those targets, and get that funding, what does that mean for you personally?**"

John paused. I waited. Then he described how reaching those outcomes would mean he could close out his career with a win so he could spend more time traveling with his family.

Phase 4 Questions: Build Out the Decision Requirements

Now that I understood the problem from John's perspective—along with why he believed it was a challenge and why it was important to fix—it was easy to customize my value proposition to him using the details that mattered to him. (More on this in the next chapter.)

"John, when you work with Unbound Growth, you can fill empty seats on your sales team without compromising quality and fit. With our two-million-plus database of sellers evaluated specifically for sales, you can recruit the best-fit sellers in a quarter of the time, and reduce attrition rates on your sales teams. We walk you and your team through each step of the hiring process to establish your specific qualifications and preferences, even when the job market is tough. That means you can quickly apply your sales hire criteria to qualified and interested sellers and sales leaders who are the best qualified fit according to objective data. Once they're hired, you'll onboard sellers in weeks instead of months because our trainers will lead your team through a repeatable and scalable onboarding process, so that you can hit your numbers in time. This reduces your risk of attrition, as every hire recommended that doesn't work out will be replaced at no charge. And our unmatched 91 percent success rate for new hires means you can more predictably scale your sales team from five to twenty-five and increase your revenue from $10 million to $100 million, so that you can secure your next phase of funding to set you up for retirement. **How do these types of decisions get made internally?"**

John shared that he would need a proposal to take to the board and founder for next week, and from there would get approval for the budget. I asked what questions he expected the board to ask that I should be including in the proposal. With that information, I asked the closing questions (which we will cover in the next chapter).

Did you notice how, during this conversation (which lasted around forty-five minutes), I didn't need to go through every possible question to get an understanding of the problem from John's perspective?

Using the sample questions in this book or in the Buyer First Workbook you have downloaded, start choosing the eleven to fourteen questions (or approximately six to eight if they are an executive, like John here) from the various question phases that are relevant to your suspected buyers. Customize them according to your research and what you know about your buyer's challenges.

Your next step is to practice asking those questions with a partner.

Practice Like a Yogi

One of the habits I developed during my health journey is daily yoga. I admired the graceful strength I saw in yogis who could do handstands and twisted balance poses that seemed to defy gravity. But I didn't think I had the time to devote to it.

Then I came across the FitOn app. It offered a wide variety of workouts—some in as little as ten minutes. I started with ten- to fifteen-minute sessions three times a week and worked my way up into more difficult and longer routines. I'm not at a full handstand—yet—but I have managed to do a full Crow Pose (imagine being upside down with your knees balanced on your triceps and your feet off the ground).

This is an example of what psychologists call deliberate practice: an intentional effort for personal improvement of performance (rather than enjoyment), often without immediate reward. (It has taken me two years of daily practice to get to the halfway point of a handstand!) In his book *Peak: Secrets from the New Science of Expertise*, the late Anders Ericsson, who was a Conradi Eminent Scholar and professor of psychology at Florida State University, tells us that how we set goals, get feedback, identify patterns, and motivate ourselves is the key to building the deliberate practice that will uplevel our skills.

When I talk about learning and changing behaviors with clients, it is all about building habits through daily practices. The frequency and intensity of your practice will depend on your environment, the gap between where you are and where you want to be, and the severity of the weakness you are trying to overcome.

As you have been doing the exercises in the previous chapters, you have been preparing yourself for what Ericsson terms "purposeful practice." This means you are focused on a specific aspect of improvement. At this point, you have an idea of which mindset is getting in your way most often, and you know the questions you should ask.

Now is the time to allow yourself to be pushed outside of your comfort zone. Reach out to colleagues, friends, or people you know well in your direct or referral list who would be willing to practice with you and give you feedback. Ask them if they would be willing to spend fifteen minutes to run through something with you and offer their advice. If they say yes or ask for more information, tell them you are working to improve your sales conversations, and you would like them to act as your buyer. If they are not currently in your buyer's role, you will need to explain more about who your buyer is and what their challenges are.

When you get into the conversation, you must set proper expectations and ask specific feedback questions to create your own safe place to practice.

For example, let's say you have identified that you don't ask enough good questions of your buyers because you are unable to stay in the moment. When you get the first clue of a problem to solve, or the buying signals, you tend to get excited and wrapped up in your own head, so you are not actively listening to your buyer. Ask your partner to try to distract you with their own interest or excitement as they answer your questions. Let them know you are only looking for feedback on this one part of the conversation. If you have time to run through the conversation more than once, ask them to throw you more difficult answers and questions.

Record these practice sessions and replay them. Focus on one aspect of the practice session to improve on, and reflect on one part that went well. Repeat your practice sessions as you focus on another aspect or area of improvement you want to make in your conversations.

Your goal should be to show up for these practice calls the same way you would for the actual call. Think of it as your dress rehearsal. As soon as your "practice buyer" has agreed to talk with you, send them the calendar invite with all the details.

Email them a day or two prior to confirm, and to ask what they want to make sure you cover.

Once on the practice call, ask them about their day so far, how they feel, or comment on something you learned about them on social or from their background information. Then, confirm how much time they have. It will be your job to manage the clock and be respectful of that time. Recap the agenda with them, starting with what they had shared was most important for them to talk about, and ask if there is anything they want to add or change to that list. (If they didn't respond to that email, ask them at the start of the call.) Then align what you are hoping to learn about to their agenda.

Let them know that you plan to save the last five minutes of the call for discussing next steps. If they gave you multiple items for the agenda, ask which one is the most important. When they answer, ask what makes that thing more important than the others on their list. Then go into the first item with your corresponding questions.

If you can find more than one partner to practice with, run through a practice session two or three times before you get on a call with a suspected buyer. It won't go perfectly, and neither will your calls with buyers, and that is okay. The goal is not perfection, but progress.

Sometimes your practice partners (and therefore your buyers) will forget their lines and say things you don't expect. That is okay too—we will handle these situations in the next chapter. For now, if someone says something unexpected or asks a question that you aren't sure how to answer, be transparent about it. Take a pause and then say, "Wow, I didn't expect to hear that, and haven't heard it before. Where does that come from for you so that I can better understand and answer?" Then write down what they say in your repository question bank as another question your future buyers might have.

It's about more than reaching your potential; it's about going beyond what you might think is possible.

If you can't find a practice partner, hire a coach who can help you navigate the obstacles you are likely to face. You can learn more about the Buyer First Practice Group at **unboundgrowth.com/buyer-first-group.**

For many of my coaching clients—and for myself—practice with others is scary. It can trigger our need for approval: we think we should be better, we worry what others will think of us if we aren't good, and we start to judge ourselves harshly before we have opened our mouths. This is the part where you get comfortable, or at least where you get used to being uncomfortable. Do you see why the personal inner work is crucial to the outer work? When you identified the hidden mindsets that were holding you back, you started on the path of deliberate practice.

Not only does regular practice and training that consistently pushes you outside your comfort zone help you change your mindset and adopt new skills, it also changes your brain by rewiring it and making new connections. It's about more than reaching your potential; it's about going beyond what you might think is possible. We'll go deeper into this in chapter 9 when we talk about your personal goals.

Close the Loop with Your Buyers

In both your practice and real-life sales conversations, the four phases of initial interview questions—uncovering the status quo, identifying why it is problem, understanding why it needs to be fixed, and discussing what a possible solution would look like and how the decision will be made—can take up the all the time you have. To conclude your initial interviews, ask your suspected buyers if they would be open-minded about hearing what you learn from their peers and what you come up with from that information. Ask how they prefer to stay in the loop.

Do they prefer email? A phone conversation? Text messages? Schedule the next call with them before you hang up. Ask if they have their calendar in front of them and offer some suggested dates and times. Ask if they are okay with you messaging them with additional questions if they come up. Do not let your follow-up fall down! If you say you will do it, do it. Otherwise, any trust and credibility you may have built is lost.

If the person you talked to doesn't want to stay in the loop, that's okay—but you are not done yet. Close out your interview by asking who the first person is who comes to mind that has also complained about this problem. Then ask:

- How do they know them?
- Do they think that the two of you would get along well?
- Would they introduce you?
- How would they prefer to introduce you? Email? Text message?
- When would they be able to make the introduction?

With each interview you do, show your appreciation for their time with you. Send a handwritten card. Give them a gift certificate to their favorite restaurant or coffee shop. Make a donation to their favorite charity in their name. This builds your relationship with your potential client or referral source, and makes them more likely to look forward to the next conversation they have with you.

Because that next conversation, or next part of the conversation, is when you go back to your interviewees to share what you came up with.

How should that conversation go? How do you take what you have learned in your research and first conversations and craft a compelling buyer first message?

Collaborative Creation Is an Evolution, Not an Event

Collaborating with your potential buyers to design and create your products and services doesn't only apply to when you first set out in your business. The reality is that your offering will never be finished, because the only constant is change. We've talked about MVP to the third power in terms of value. Think of your initial offering as a different kind of MVP—Minimally Viable Products (and services) that evolve over time.

When I first started my sales consultancy, I did one-on-one coaching over a conference line and through email support. After a year, I started to notice that sellers often had a difficult time recalling exactly what happened on their calls, so I told them to record them and send them to me to review. Not long after that, companies started using call recording technology and called it coaching. I could have seen this as a threat to what I was doing, but by asking my coaching clients and prospective clients how they were using this new technology, what they liked about it, what was a challenge, and what they wished they could do, I was able to get ahead of the disruption by including call reviews in my one-on-one coaching and by eventually adding it as a module for management training.

By including my buyers in the process of creating my offering, I was able to innovate and differentiate from my competitors, and stay ahead of an industry trend. You will be more likely to anticipate market trends and industry changes when you collaborate with your buyers, because you will be more in tune with their needs.

That means there is no such thing as perfection, and no reason to wait to start the process of selling it with your potential clients and customers.

What you come up with is your beta, or pilot, offering, and the initial list that you come up with are your early adopters to test it with. But before you start telling everyone about it, you will need to make sure you can maintain the feedback loop that will enable you to continue to evolve that offering.

Collaboration with buyers will impact you and your business both now and in the future as you grow, from your company culture and policies to how you adapt to your market and industry changes.

You now have a toolbox full of strategies and techniques to change the way you think about selling and how to start the conversations with potential buyers and referral sources. Now, how do you move from uncovering a challenge, the status quo, and commitment to change to the purchase of a solution?

KEY ACTIONS AND TAKEAWAYS

We place more value on things we have co-created. So when you ask collaborative questions of your buyers, they place more value on the solution because it is one you have come up with together rather than one you have prescribed to them without their input. When you follow the Buyer First Rules of Engagement and make it all about them with customized questions and content, demonstrate a quantifiable impact, and use emotional descriptors to compare and contrast options, you engage with them in ways that they will find more valuable and credible.

Start by preparing and planning the questions that are targeted to who your buyer is and where they are in their process. Practice asking and answering your questions in a conversation with a partner who will role-play with you. The more you practice, the more confident you will become and the more prepared you will be to sell with your buyers in a meaningful way.

Share your #buyerfirst questions with me on social or via email for feedback on sentiment and structure.

7

SELL WITH YOUR BUYERS

Value is in the eye of the buyer.
LISA DENNIS

TOM WAS THE only salesperson in his family-owned software company. Like the rest of his family, Tom worked as an EMT, and developed software to help emergency service professionals track their incident and patient reports remotely so they can report quickly and accurately to hospitals and physicians for patient care and billing. Their software could truly help save lives. Tom didn't merely know about this industry and profession, he lived it. He knew every challenge and obstacle that EMTs have to face daily.

It was this curse of knowledge that made Tom's conversations with potential buyers boring (his word, not mine). As a business owner, what you do is often your life's work—something you have studied, practiced, and become an expert in. As a seller, your company has likely tried to drill into you the ins and outs of their industry and solution. This is good in the sense that it helps us understand, but bad because it makes it all too easy to start telling our buyers what we know instead of collaborating with them.

In case I haven't mentioned it recently: Selling isn't something we do *to* others, it is something we do *with* them.

When Tom hired me to coach him, he was frustrated that, while he was doing a lot of demos, for some reason not a lot of people were buying. Wasn't it obvious to them how this would solve their problems?

I had Tom record his demo calls and, as I watched and listened to them, the problem became obvious. Here is how it would go:

> Hi Frank, nice to meet you. How are you today? Great. So, Andrea tells me that you are the director of services for ACME Emergency Services. Do you know of Great Falls Ambulance? Yeah—they are a customer of ours close to you. So, let me show you what our software can do. It's a super simple application downloaded onto your machines—whether it is a tablet or desktop. You log in here. To start a new patient record, all you do is click here...

You could tell by the tone of Tom's voice that he had done this thousands of times. At the end of the forty-five-minute step-by-step walk-through of the software, Tom would get down to talking price and when they might want to buy.

In addition to reviewing his calls, my team used the Objective Management Group (OMG) data to evaluate Tom's sales skills and areas of improvement. The report results suggested that he was making a lot of assumptions, not asking enough good questions, pitching too soon, and, because of all this, wasn't able to uncover compelling reasons for buyers to make a change, and wasn't able to show value to them.

What Tom didn't realize is that he was selling *to* them and demoing *at* them, but not doing either of these things *with* them. They didn't need to be there. (Again, his words, not mine, which he offered after listening to the call recordings.)

After I worked with Tom for six months, his demos went from nap-inducing product pitches to excited conversations between two colleagues planning a new project.

What actions, techniques, and tactics did Tom have to take? What does the science say about that? What behaviors and mindsets did he need to become aware of and consciously work to change to do it consistently?

At this point, you have already done a lot. In chapter 4, you identified and started work on the biggest mindset block toward sales you have. Next, in chapter 5, you found your people, did research on them, and reached out to set up a conversation. With chapter 6, you brainstormed and practiced your questions in role-play conversations to uncover your buyer's Most Valuable Problems and your Most Valuable Product. After that conversation, you listened to your recordings to figure out what went well and what you still need to know or work on.

You have learned how to understand your buyer's current reality—to a degree. Now is the time to gather what you have learned about your buyer and use it to demonstrate how you can help them.

That doesn't mean it's time to make it all about you, which is another big hole most business owners and sellers fall into. Just as Tom did, they can go into a monologue of what they can do for the buyer.

And buyers tune out. They've heard this all before.

This is where you will stand out and differentiate yourself from the competition.

How? Is this the part where we dig into value proposition and elevator pitches? What is the best way to structure messaging that will appeal to your buyers?

Remember: selling is an exchange of value. It is something you do *with* other people. This next conversation, or part of the conversation, is where you demonstrate that you have heard your buyer and understand their current situation and future goals, and where you align how you can help them get there. This is still a two-way conversation—a collaboration. Remember chapter 4 and the disastrous allergy incident that happened when I was a waitress? Just as the chef and I in the restaurant should have confirmed with each other that we had heard correctly, you need to confirm with your buyers that you have heard them, and they have heard you.

You may be a bit apprehensive for this next part of the conversation with your buyer—which makes preparation and practice all that much more important.

Continue to Practice with Your Partner

I used to have debilitating stage fright. When I was asked to speak to audiences, my anxiety would get so high that I wouldn't be able to sleep for days leading up to the event. I would feel nauseous the day of; I'd sound like a version of Minnie Mouse on stage because my voice would get constricted, and my hands would shake to the point that I would drop things.

But I made myself do it because I believed that the message of putting buyers first was worth spreading.

When I was introduced to Heroic Public Speaking (HPS) and their mission to change the world one speech at a time, I thought they would help me feel less anxious and sick to my stomach on stage, and I would learn to impact people in a way that they would remember (and would then want to hire me).

What I didn't realize is that HPS's rehearsal process would change both how I showed up on stage and how I showed up for everything. Cofounder Michael Port writes in his book *Steal the Show* that the craft of acting is applicable to all the things we do in life, because of what you learn from the practice of it.

By writing down what I wanted to say, saying it out loud, editing it, and rehearsing it, I built my confidence and my communication skills. And you can do the same with your sales conversations. Here is how.

Prepare

Which part of the conversation are you most nervous or unsure about? That is the part to rehearse with your coach or practice partner. At this stage of your conversation, or practice, you may find that you get anxious or nervous—which is completely normal. However, it is important to manage and channel that energy, or it can easily take you out of the present moment with your buyers. This is the part of the conversation where it gets more difficult because you may get objections and feel uncomfortable talking about money.

Here are a few things you can do prior to your practice and real calls to better manage these emotions and learn to stay in the moment. (Some are so silly that you may end up laughing at yourself!)

First, give yourself ten to fifteen minutes prior to any sales conversations to do some warm-up exercises. In her book *Act Like a Sales Pro*, Julie Hansen shares some of the routines that professional speakers, actors, and performers go through to both warm up their bodies and voices and to center and ground their nerves. It's not that they don't get nervous (we sure do!), it's that these routines help them channel that nervous energy into something powerful.

One of Hansen's rituals that I have adopted is to warm up my voice, typically while in the shower because the steam helps to moisturize the vocal cords. Professional singers and speakers know that frequent talking doesn't warm up your vocal muscles on its own. To maintain a calm and steady voice, repeat these sounds and phrases:

- "ba-ba-ba, pa-pa-pa"
- "ta-ta-ta, da-da-da"
- "ka-ka-ka, ga-ga-ga"

To learn to articulate clearly, repeat these short tongue twisters:

- "sushi chef"
- "toy boat"
- "world wide web"
- "round the rough and rugged rock the ragged rascal ran"
- "unique New York"
- "while one blue bear bled black, the other black bear bled blue"
- "how much wood could a woodchuck chuck if a woodchuck could chuck wood?"

In addition to Hansen's warm-up, I do breathing exercises that I learned from yoga and meditation. Place your hand under your ribcage and breathe through your mouth until you feel it move. Think of your breath as an ocean wave: breathe in for four counts, hold it for four counts, and then breathe out through your mouth for eight counts.

Tension is an energy suck that robs us of focus. It is held in our bodies, most commonly in the neck and shoulders. To release it, sit in a straight-backed chair, close your eyes, and examine where you feel tight in your body. Focus on one body part at a time, starting from your shoulders and moving down. Lift your shoulders up to your ears, rotate them backward, and, when you find the point of tension, hold that muscle tightly for ten seconds, then let it go. Repeat throughout your body, tensing and releasing until you don't notice any tension left. (This works well if you are having a hard time getting to sleep at night.)

Before I get on a stage, or if I am nervous before an important call, I do what Hansen calls the rag doll exercise. Stand up straight, inhale, and then on the exhale start to roll your body down. Shake your arms from side to side, keeping your neck loose. Inhale and slowly roll your body back up, one vertebra at a time. Then shake your legs: standing up on one leg, shake the other loosely, then change sides. This can help relieve tension and nerves, and help you connect with your body—which in turn helps you stay in the present moment with your audience or buyer.

In my public speaking training, I learned that people will react to your facial expressions. This is an especially important exercise if you are going to be face-to-face or on video. Scrunch your face up as if you sucked on a lemon, hold it for a moment, and then release, making your face as wide as you can, as if you were feeling surprised. Then, lift your eyebrows up and down quickly, and hold them up. Stretch your jaw by opening your mouth as wide as you can and then rotating your lower jaw around, stopping wherever you feel tension. Move your lips from side to side and in and out. Stick out your tongue and move it in circles as well as in and out. Blow raspberries at yourself, as you would with a baby.

Pause

In addition to these daily exercises, there are things you can do in the moment to help you to stay present when you might otherwise get lost in your thoughts.

When buyers say phrases that get us excited, such as "This sounds awesome!" or "I can't wait to tell my team about this," it can be easy to get wrapped up in that excitement. I would keep a hair elastic around my wrist, and when I heard these types of phrases or get into a scenario where I was finding myself distracted or my mind was wandering, I would snap it to keep myself in the present moment. Others use tricks like pressing their middle finger and thumb together, or doing some other physical reminder to come back to the present.

A lot can happen in three to five seconds. Your heart rate can change, your breath can slow down, and you can have a dozen different thoughts. When you find yourself mentally spinning plates after someone says something that surprises you, don't react. Pause. Ponder. Be curious. Then repeat what you think you heard and ask a question that clarifies or defines it. Too often I hear sellers on calls who immediately jump to answer a question or objection, and often their answer has little to do with what the buyer said. They are reacting to what they think they heard—too fast. Oftentimes, a pause is uncomfortable, and we want to fill that gap with something. Well, so do your buyers. Let them fill that gap, because what they think matters more.

These short-term tactics are useful in the moment, but only to a degree. To truly manage your emotions, revisit and follow the mindset practices and strategies you learned in chapter 4.

Follow Up with Next Steps

Now, what do you need to do in this next part of the conversation? What do you need to practice with your partner? If this is a separate conversation at another day or time, follow the same steps of sending the calendar invite, confirming it at a day or two prior, and summarizing the first conversation (including the agenda for the upcoming one), and then asking for their input and feedback.

Once you get on the call, confirm again how much time you have available to talk. If you are still on the call when the arranged time is nearly over, do a check-in: do they have a hard stop, or are they willing to stay longer if you need more time? Then, summarize the highlights of the previous conversation and the corresponding agenda for the next part of your discussion. This may seem redundant, but remember: we are all busy people who need reminders, and the span of a few days can bring up new questions and concerns. Things change fast.

Now, what is the best way to introduce your solution and continue to collaborate with them?

Share What You Came Up With

To find out what type of messaging truly works best at this stage, I turned to B2B DecisionLabs, who tested traditional value messaging frameworks in a behavioral experiment with 400 B2B buyers. The types of messaging they tested included a features-based message that listed capabilities that solve a buyer's challenge or problem, a benefits-based message that described the benefits of each capability so that buyers would understand what each feature can do for them, and "superlative" messaging, which uses terms such as "all-in-one," "streamlined," or "integrated."

However, it was the fourth type of messaging that buyers described as the most preferred, credible, convincing, and most likely to lead them to buy. These "telling details" are specific to the business problem, how the capability solves it, and the value that it has. Because it is so detailed, this messaging is much longer than traditional value propositions. Do you recall how, in the previous chapter, I described Unbound Growth's capabilities with John after understanding his business issues and impact?

> When you work with Unbound Growth, you can fill empty seats on your sales team without compromising quality and fit. With our two-million-plus database of sellers evaluated specifically for sales, you can recruit the best-fit sellers in a quarter of the time, and reduce attrition rates on your sales teams. We walk you and your team through each step of the hiring process to establish your specific qualifications and preferences, even when the job market is tough. That means you can quickly apply your sales hire criteria to qualified

The devil is in the details. Specifics make the vision of success more believable.

> and interested sellers and sales leaders who are the best qualified fit according to objective data. Once they're hired, you'll onboard sellers in weeks instead of months because our trainers will lead your team through a repeatable and scalable onboarding process, so that you can hit your numbers in time. This reduces your risk of attrition, as every hire recommended that doesn't work out will be replaced at no charge. And our unmatched 91 percent success rate for new hires means you can more predictably scale your sales team from five to twenty-five and increase your revenue from $10 million to $100 million, so that you can secure your next phase of funding to set you up for retirement.

Can you guess why this type of messaging won out—by a lot—across all the variables in the study?

First, it is buyer first focused and uses language such as "you can" and "that means" to frame capabilities. That makes it all about the buyer, not your features and benefits.

Second, it is specific and quantifiable, which helps to make the capability more credible.

Because this type of messaging is buyer focused, specific, and quantifiable, more than 90 percent of buyers tested said it was more valuable to them.

The devil is in the details. Specifics make the vision of success more believable.

Yes, that means it takes time to develop and deliver. It also means that you must be very good at active listening and asking good clarifying questions—which you have been working on since chapter 4. Without that, how could you possibly know which details matter? Don't add more words for the hell of it—have a point, and a point that matters to your buyers. If the additional information doesn't add clarity, then you don't need it.

This is the opportunity you have: to create connections between you and your buyers. Collaboration with your buyer in the conversation acts the same way as when you share a memory with someone, and they add their own recollections to that memory. We can create a more complete picture together than we can alone. This is yet another way to sell with your buyers, not to them.

If you have actual products to demonstrate—whether it is software or a real-life demo—you can work this type of messaging into your demonstration within the framework of a business problem, how the capability solves it, and the value that has to offer.

Summarize what you heard and remembered as an important problem from the first conversation, and then show them the relevant feature that solves that problem. Throughout your demonstration, ask questions about how your solution compares to how they do it now, what impact it would have on their day-to-day, or how it matches up against the other options they are considering. For example, "You shared that tracking where your customers came from was an issue because you don't know where your marketing investments are paying off. That means you may be missing part of the market because you are spending too much money elsewhere. If that doesn't change before the start of next year and you lose market share, you won't hit the revenue goals your investors are expecting. Because you have a small team, you don't have the resources to handle complicated technology, and, right now, your tracking is done between several people and spreadsheets. When you use ABC to track your campaigns, you only need to <etc.>. How does this feature compare to how you are doing it now?"

Go through the list of challenges you uncovered in the previous part of the conversation and how they impact their goal, and then demonstrate or explain your capability, followed by open-ended questions to get their feedback.

Often, buyers will come to you after having done a lot of their own research and all they want is to see your solution and pricing. Meet them where they are by incorporating the first few phases of questions into your demo. For example, when they say they want to see a particular feature, as you open your demo, ask what makes that feature most important now, how it happens today, and what impact that has. Then show them what they asked for and follow up by asking how it is different from their current status quo.

Stop Handling Objections

This is all well and good, but how does it play out in real life? I'm not going to tell you that customizing this messaging with the details you learned in your previous conversation will get you new clients right away. You may find that as soon as you start asking about money—the proof of the exchange of value—your buyers still come up with objections or concerns, or want to think it over. What then?

In that study of 120 entrepreneurs I mentioned earlier in this book, Vincent Onyemah and his colleagues found that handling the objections of potential customers was the biggest problem that business founders have with the actual mechanics of selling.

I have seen both professional sellers and business owners (myself included) stumble when client objections come up. This is where selling with buyers is the most difficult, because of the defense mechanisms in their mind that cause them (and you) to react poorly.

Do you remember my coaching client Michael Douglas—the one who was working on managing his emotions in the moment? This is what was happening to Michael when he heard buyer comments such as "This is a great tool!" or objections such as "We need to do our due diligence with two other competitors." He would get excited or frustrated and start pitching and telling them why they should or shouldn't. He didn't know what to do to handle these objections.

I asked him what would happen if he stopped handling them.

"What do you mean, 'stop handling them'? How can I ignore them? The deal will never happen otherwise!"

I challenged him by asking if he had a deal to lose at this point. Michael begrudgingly agreed that no, he didn't have a deal. I explained that I wasn't saying he should ignore the objection, only that he should stop "handling" it. I encouraged him instead to seek to understand where the objection came from and ask more questions about it, such as:

- That is a valid point—can you tell me what that means for you?
- Has this happened before, and not gone well?
- If that happens here, how do you want to handle it?

For many, objections arise from a fear they have. Remember: change is hard and decisions are made emotionally. This is where you may need to help your buyer reduce their fear of change by reframing it with them.

Cognitive reframing is a psychological technique that helps people gain new perspectives by identifying and disputing irrational or negative thoughts and changing how they view things to a positive alternative. There are two steps to this: first, validate their perspective; then, offer a positive perspective to counter their negative one.

This is not about lying or spinning the truth—far from it. Reframing is a technique therapists use with trauma patients. It doesn't change their circumstance but rather their outlook on it. You can shift any negative to a positive. What follows are a few examples of how I might reframe someone saying "It's too expensive" for my hiring programs.

Reframe 1: Compare and contextualize available options. What could they do and how will that impact the future? (Remember, doing nothing is always an option—and the one that is most likely to happen!)

> Yes, this is a significant investment in cost and time. You could delay the decision, but, based on what you said, your cost of a failed sales hire is, at a rate of three turnovers for every ten you hire, $300,000. A $15,000 investment now to screen out those poor fits is a one-time cost of $1,500 per salesperson. Would you rather pay $300,000 in six months, or $1,500 per hire now to ensure that you are hiring the best candidates for your future growth?

Reframe 2: Restate the cost of consequences. What is their desired gain and fear of loss?

> Yes, you are right. This is not a small investment. What about the return that you are looking for? Is a $15,000 investment to reach that additional $1.5 million in revenue worth it? What if you don't make this investment? What if you overlook your next top salesperson and they end up working for the competition? Or, worse, what if you hire the wrong salesperson again and they miss their quotas and leave you scrambling to meet the revenue targets that your investors expect?

Reframe 3: Align with content they shared. What do they believe about their goals and how can you align to it?

> I understand that this is a large investment to you. You shared that you want to nurture a culture of excellence and learning in your sales organization in order to consistently break through revenue targets—but, more importantly, that you want to put your customer first in all interactions. If you hire

the wrong salespeople on the front lines because you underinvested in the process, those few bad hires can damage morale and your customer experience. This solution is proven to help hire the right salespeople for high-performing sales organizations like yours.

With these frameworks, you can help your buyers think differently about their problems and gain a new perspective, which research shows is what buyers value most in salespeople they want to work with.

This was hard for Michael at first, but when he did the daily practices you read about in chapter 4 to learn to stay in the moment, he found that not only was he better able to manage his emotions during the sales process of working through objections with his buyers, but he was also more present with his family and less distracted in his daily life.

But objections are not the only obstacle that can happen. Often this is where the door is opened to negotiate as well, especially as you bring up the topic of money.

Talk about the Money

In your previous conversation with your buyer, you learned what results they expect, by when, and what impact those results would have. If you haven't asked about the money yet, now is the time. Otherwise, how can either of you understand whether the value of the results is greater than the investment they would need to make to get there? Here are some questions you can ask:

- How much do you think it should cost to fix/do this?
- You shared that you wanted to reach X in revenue by solving this. Is it worth an investment of Y to get X?

You will not be an effective negotiator if you cannot manage your own emotions.

- What about your company's purchasing process? When we decide what the best solution is to get you there, who do you need to get funding from? What about legal and technology? How long does that typically take? What questions will they have? When should we be getting them involved?
- And for you, when you have bought solutions like this before, what steps did you need to take? How long have you given yourself to get through those steps? What obstacles do you foresee coming up? How do you want to work through those things if they happen?

This may be where you need to be prepared to negotiate. If that makes you a bit nervous, you are not alone. Eighty-seven percent of sellers struggle with negotiations, according to our data research with OMG—the only things they struggle with more are closing and Consultative Selling. This is concerning, but not surprising, since many of the attributes needed are similar—such as being goal oriented, and being able to actively listen and ask clarification questions, control their emotions, stay in the moment, not let their need for approval get in the way, recover from rejections quickly, and sell on value—and being comfortable discussing money. And for negotiating, the ability to seek a win/win and a willingness to walk away are both important.

Unfortunately, because most sellers struggle here, they can resort to discounts and false deadlines to try to "create urgency" in buyers to get them to take action. But we don't create urgency in our buyers, we uncover it *with* them. A discount is not urgency; it is a recipe for churn later because buyers don't see the value in the solution.

Which brings me to my other pet peeve about negotiating: it's not simply about money and price. There are terms to be settled, product features, support, all kinds of things we negotiate.

Unfortunately, if you see negotiation as a battle, this can bring up your fear of rejection and your preference to avoid conflict, leading you to give in as a way to avoid those things. That inhibits your ability to communicate clearly, and to be present in a way that will allow you to see the style of the other person and adapt your own style accordingly.

Just as with all sales: it is not rational, it is emotional. It's not about ROI, or spreadsheets, or price—it is about emotions. Fear, loss, self-image... all of it. You will not be an effective negotiator if you cannot manage your own emotions. Just as they tell you on an airplane: put your own oxygen mask on before you try to help someone else with theirs.

To shift our mindsets here, we need to understand what biases are at play. One of my favorite books on negotiations is by Fotini Iconomopoulos: *Say Less, Get More.* She shares that in negotiations there is the endowment bias, where we overvalue something we own and undervalue something being sold. Not to mention all the prejudices we have because of our own experiences and preferences.

How do we overcome these biases for ourselves, and work around those of other people?

Knowledge is power, as Iconomopoulos says in her book. She lists four ways to get that knowledge: pauses, research, questions, and sharing something about yourself. Not only does the knowledge you gain from these strategies give you more power in your "negotiation battery," as she puts it, it gives you confidence as well.

If you think back to chapter 4, you will recall the importance of pausing and how it can help you manage your emotions. When you uncover something your buyers either don't know or haven't fully considered, it both adds value and gives you power in your negotiations. This is another critical role of the research you read about in chapter 5, and how that helps you develop good, targeted questions, as you learned how to do in chapter 6.

Another important aspect to negotiations is setting specific timelines—for the results, and for the sales call itself. A scheduled thirty-minute "closing" meeting might start off reasonably relaxed, but as the clock ticks, the pressure can build to "get this done." You start talking faster and louder, and in trying to get it done fast, you give up a lot.

Rather than rush, this is another place to use the pause. Iconomopoulos writes that when you pause, the pressure to perform goes to the other person, giving you time to control your emotions.

Ultimately, you must always check on your willingness to walk out of a negotiation. Sometimes, the longer the negotiation, the more tired you and the buyer become. I've seen situations where a buyer will stick to their guns and refuse to give anything or let you "win," no matter what—even though they are harming themselves by doing so. This is another example of a commitment bias: *I have invested so much time, effort, and energy into this—I can't give up now.* You see this when we won't dump the toxic partner or quit the bad job or fire the unsuccessful employee. Do not wait to work out the details later; do the details before you get to any negotiation. Have a clear offer first.

The other part of being willing to walk is being clear on your goals—what you want to achieve. With that, you can ask about their goals and find the common ground.

When making an ask, give context and tell them why you are making that ask, framed in something they care about. "I'm sure you don't want to have to wait for support to get back to you when you have an urgent issue, which is why we charge for premium support to get you back up and running no matter what the issue is."

In the actual negotiation, their least appealing option is your most appealing one, so you have to figure out with them what the range is and where your ranges overlap. If you can sell it between two and six and they can buy it between one and four, then you have a common range of two to four. This is what you are able to receive, and what they are able to give. Start with the anchor option—the most extreme end of your range. When you get the response, you then know what the end of their range is. If they don't tell you, ask. And let the dance begin.

Once you have the money and the preferred terms sorted out, it is time for the big ask. Will they buy from you?

Close with Three Questions

One of the most shocking OMG statistics that I share with business and sales leaders is that 95 percent of sellers worldwide struggle with closing. This is the number one reason that clients come to me for sales training and coaching: so they can close more business. The challenge is that they believe there is a way to close the business that will make everything come together—but what many don't realize is that the close starts the moment they say hello.

There is a way to ask for the business that is still a collaboration with your buyer.

Remember Dave Kurlan, founder of OMG, whose data informs many of the statistics I have shared with you? In his book *Baseline Selling*, he shares what he calls "The Natural Close." These three simple questions to ask for the business enable you to get to the point in a way that is a natural conclusion to the sequence of questions and collaboration you have been doing with your buyers.

The first of Kurlan's three questions to your buyer is: "Do you believe I understand everything necessary about your world and the issue/opportunity you are trying to solve for?" When you ask this question and get anything other than a yes, then your collaboration is not complete. If your buyer says, "I think so..." or "Maybe..." then your next question needs to be: "What is missing; what do we still need to cover?"

If your buyer answers yes, they do believe you understand their world and their issues, your next question is: "Do you believe I/we have the expertise/solution to help?" Another way to ask this is: "On a scale of 1 to 7, how confident are you that this solution will solve the issue?" Again, if you get anything other than a yes or a 7, dig into that. If it's not a 7, ask what they believe is missing that would make it a 7.

The final question is to ask if they want your help. If the answer is not a yes, ask what you missed, or what they believe the obstacle is.

Ideally, once you have a yes to all of these questions, you are then able to put everything that you and your buyer have discussed and agreed on into a proposal. When working with my buyers, I set the expectation that this a draft document we will refine together to save us both the time of going back and forth. I deliver the draft proposal in a meeting where we work out the details together in writing.

Application in the Real World

Powered by Hue was founded by Sylvan Guo, Janvi Shah, and Nicole Clay to help consumers who buy makeup online find the right shades for them.

I first met Sylvan at Harvard Business School when she went through the sales course I was coaching for in the Entrepreneurial MBA program. As the person in charge of sales for their startup, she was eager to learn new skills to get their first customer, but she wasn't sure where to start. She felt that her biggest challenge to getting their first customer was that they didn't have a product to demonstrate. Who would buy into a technology that didn't exist yet? All they had were some mockups to show.

During a coaching session, we talked about who her buyer would be. She shared that cosmetics companies often offer return policies, which can get expensive and can damage the customer experience. In addition to that, cart abandonment is a dirty word in e-commerce: people put something in their online shopping cart, then bail out before they complete the purchase. When that happens, it can be difficult to get those shoppers back to the website to complete the transaction. Sometimes smart buyers know that the company will send them an email with an extra discount as incentive to get them to come back and make the purchase (ahem—I know I'm guilty of this!). All this increases the cost of sales for these online brands, which often operate on narrow margins. Sylvan's technology could change the way people buy cosmetics online by giving them the confidence that they have selected the right shade for their skin tone.

"This is all great to know, but who are the people in those companies who are responsible for these things and who do they report to?" I asked.

After she shared their roles and titles, I asked who she and her partners knew in the industry. What connections did they have who could introduce them to the right people? How does she know them? When was the last time she spoke with them? After coaching her to simply reach out and ask how things were in their world, and to see if they would be open to catching up, she told me she was doubtful it could work. It seemed to go against all the sales teachings she had studied. "Don't I need a product to demo before I reach out to people? Or at the very least the right value proposition and pitch? Will they really want to spend time on catching up?"

I reminded Sylvan about the importance of relationships and how we buy based on emotion, not on facts, demos, and

ROI. This is why people will stand in line in the cold for hours to buy the newest iPhone, or for tickets to see their favorite band. And some people place an even greater value on a product or service if they have participated in creating it. Remember, when we can collaborate in the making of something we are going to use, we value it more. I encouraged Sylvan to lean into that and consider what contacts and companies are innovating in that space. Who could be an eager early adopter wanting to get in on the ground floor to shape the product to their needs?

Using the messaging in chapter 5 to find and reach out to people, Sylvan ended up connecting with several beauty brands whose digital executives were eager to offer their features, wish-lists, and visions for her upcoming product.

During her next coaching session, we brainstormed the questions she needed to ask from chapter 6 to collaborate with those executives and digital managers. Sylvan and her partners were excited that they were having conversations that were helping them fine-tune their product—but they still wondered: would people be willing to pay for a product that wasn't done yet? I shared with her the research on the IKEA Effect and coached her to use the Anchoring Effect to position the price.

After using the negotiation and closing techniques I've described in this chapter, Powered by Hue found their first beta customer. Using the mindsets and skill set techniques you have learned in this book, she was able to align their capabilities to the needs of that buyer—before the product was fully built out.

A few months after her semester ended, she emailed me to tell me that they had acquired a few more beta customers, and had completely revamped their product based on what they learned during their pilot.

Today, Powered by Hue continues to use the strategies and techniques described in this book to innovate their product around their buyer. They have expanded their contracts with their beta customers and are taking on new customers as they scale their business.

When you do the work to put your buyer first, you can get your first or next customer too. Sylvan was motivated to prove herself and reach a specific milestone. She embraced the buyer first mindset that selling isn't something you do *to* others, it's something you do *with* them. She did the work and continues to challenge herself.

What about you? What fires you up every day to make the world different, better? You may already realize that this is hard work. It does get easier and faster the more you work the process and challenge yourself.

But how can you motivate yourself to go outside of your comfort zone regularly to see the results you seek?

KEY ACTIONS AND TAKEAWAYS

We make our decisions not by logic and reason but by emotion and feeling. Our buyers decide what to do as soon as they discover a problem. When you research and prepare your questions and then practice them, you are learning to manage your emotions so that you can help your buyer navigate theirs throughout the decision-making process. Preparation and practice are crucial to being in the present moment with your buyers so that are you able to actively listen, which leads to the best questions to ask.

Begin to develop the skills you need by preparing the questions to ask based on your buyer, their role, and where they are in the process. Write them down, say them out loud, and practice with a partner who will give you targeted and relevant feedback. Share your #buyerfirst quick wins with me on social media or email. When you do, you will increase your own confidence in your ability to sell with your buyers.

8

FEED THE FIRE IN YOUR BELLY

One who has a why to live for
can bear almost any how.
FRIEDRICH NIETZSCHE

WHEN YOU DO the work described in this book, the process will help you change the way you think and act as a seller with your buyers. I believe that anyone is capable of transformative change. I see it every day. When clients come to me with a purpose they are pursuing—or, as I call it, a fire in their belly—something that is urging them to do whatever it takes to reach a goal, it is as if I am watching my kids open presents on Christmas morning. Because when we have a purpose, that opens opportunities to us that we might not have seen before.

But I see those who won't change too. They aren't happy with where they are, but they aren't willing to do anything about it—either out of fear (*What if I can't do it?*), stubbornness (*I will work harder, hustle, and grind until it happens!*), or a perhaps a sense of entitlement (*It shouldn't be this hard for me; why do I have to be the one to change? Why is it so much easier for everyone else?*). We instinctively know that transformation doesn't happen until someone wants it. No amount of incentives, shame, or consequences will make a person alter their thinking and behaviors if they don't want to. There will always be a reason or excuse why they can't.

The hardest part of my job is letting some people fail so that they can be open to change. If I were to rescue them every time, why would they do anything different? This is a tough lesson to learn as a new manager, parent, or friend.

Which is why I say, with as much love as I can convey on a page, I hope you failed at some of the exercises in this book. Because if you did, and you are still here on this page with me, then there might be a fire in your belly that won't let you quit.

And if you want to quit—and, if not yet, then certainly at some point you will—then this chapter and the next two are for you.

When you are asked what you want, what you deeply and truly want, how do you answer? Is the "why" behind your goals clear to you? Or are you doing what you think you should, or what everyone tells you that you should? Understanding the source of your motivation is critical to start your behavior change and make it stick long term.

It is true for me, it is true for you, and it is true for your potential buyers. When you have the courage to ask and answer the question of what drives *you* to make a change, it will be all that much easier to do the same with your buyers—and to not accept fluffy answers. Because when your buyer is not motivated to make a change, the best seller in the world won't be able to get them to buy a solution for a problem that will make that change happen. If you care more about it than they do, that should be a red flag for you.

You see, you aren't selling yourself, your product, or your solution. What selling is truly about is determining whether your buyer wants to make a change. They might need to, but until they want to, they likely won't. This is why selling isn't something we do *to* them—it must be something we do *with* them.

Sales is the lifeblood of any business. Without it, there is no business. You know this—it is why you are reading this book: to get more clients and customers. We need money, money, money. Where is it going to come from?

But when I ask business owners and salespeople about what they want, the answer is typically more time with family, less stress over the things they can't control, and more confidence that they are doing the right things.

What we think we need and what we want are not always the same things.

The motivation of more customers and clients may not be enough for you to make a long-lasting mindset and behavioral change. That means you will need to dig deeper into what you want and why, and not only what you need right now. Because if the only reason you are doing this is to make more money, you might be better off going to work for someone else. And that's okay. But if that is not an acceptable option for you, read on.

Sales is the toughest job there is, and being a business owner is tougher than selling someone else's product or service. When you are selling someone else's stuff and they say no, it's not you they are rejecting. (If you are a salesperson in a company reading this, remember that!)

This is one reason why selling yourself as a business owner is so much harder, and why it is the most important skill for us to master. But business owners are not the only ones who are struggling with finding their purpose and finding more business.

Debunking Motivational Myths

Mauricio was a coaching client who worked at a mid-sized software company in Boston, and was referred to me by his new sales manager, David. I agreed to meet with Mauricio, and when I asked why he was seeking sales coaching, he had a ready answer: "Well, I need to make my quota and get off my performance improvement plan. Then I want to make it into President's Club, which will set me up to get into management."

"So what? Everyone wants that," I responded.

Judging from the long pause on the other end of the phone, I don't think he expected or appreciated that answer.

"Well, I am not everyone!" he shot back, his voice a little heated.

"Of course not. What about getting into President's Club and eventually into management is important to you?"

Another long pause. I waited.

"Okay, David said you were the tough love type, so let's get real here. This is my first sales job, and I thought I would crush it, but now I am wondering if I am cut out for it," Mauricio said, his tone going from hot to quiet. "This job was a dream come true for me. It's tough to get in here. Everyone knows that if you can make it here, you can make it anywhere. When I got hired, I thought that this was my chance to prove myself to my dad. He's a successful businessman, and eventually I want to be able to take over his business. But I don't want it handed to me. I need to show him, myself, and everyone else that I can do this on my own. I can't let him, or myself, down. But if I don't make my numbers in the next few months, I am going to get canned."

"Now we are getting somewhere!" I replied. I agreed to work with Mauricio, and over the next six months we addressed the mindsets that were getting in the way of him doing the things he knew he should do, and how he could maintain his motivation when things became frustrating and he wanted to give up.

But if you are a business owner, or a seller who doesn't have a supportive manager to coach, motivate, and keep you accountable, how can you do this for yourself? As a business owner, you won't be fired and be forced to go find a job, will you? No, this is about the survival of your company and your dream.

Why was keeping his job not enough of a goal for Mauricio? And why is getting more customers and clients and making more money not enough of a goal for you? If losing your job or not paying your bills isn't enough to motivate a change, what is?

To dig into where your true source of motivation is, let's first debunk two motivational myths so you can see your own source of motivation more clearly.

Motivational Myth Number 1: Money

While I was lying awake at night in tears over how to buy groceries and Christmas presents for my kids, it wasn't enough for me to change the way I thought about sales and to behave differently. I still couldn't seem to make myself do the things I thought I should. You want to get more clients and customers too, right?

But are you motivated by the money? Or by something deeper? Money is emotional, and so it can be easy to assume that money will motivate us.

It is a common belief that successful sellers are motivated by money. It seems an obvious and easy answer. That doesn't make it true. In fact, according to Objective Management Group (OMG) data from over two million sellers worldwide, the majority of the world's top sales performers are not primarily motivated by money.

Let that sink in for a moment. The best salespeople in the world are not motivated by money alone.

There are three main types of motivation that I measure for when using this data to work with business owners, sellers, and sales leaders: extrinsic, intrinsic, and altruistic. And it is not that one style of motivation is good, and the other two are bad; it is that they are different and therefore impact us differently. It is also important to remember that our motivation style will typically be a blend of all three, and will depend on the task or things we are trying to accomplish. For now, we are talking strictly about the motivation to be successful in your sales role. And, according to the data, only 23 percent of salespeople are extrinsically motivated—meaning, they are driven by rewards, money, and materialistic gain such as a fast car or a new house.

Despite the data showing that money isn't the primary motivator for most sellers, the most common incentive used in sales teams is extrinsic motivation—i.e., money, in the form of cash incentives and bonuses. It seems ironic to me that we assume money motivates us, yet so many of us have issues in relation to money. As a business owner, you want and need more clients to make more money, and that is great. But is that enough to make some hard behavioral changes? Will that get you to cold-call ten people? Or reach out to that hard-to-connect-with executive over and over again? Or put aside some long-held beliefs that you grew up with?

Now, you might be thinking that if only 23 percent of salespeople are extrinsically motivated, then that must include the top 10 percent of salespeople, right? I thought so too. I thought wrong. When I analyzed how the top 10 percent of sellers worldwide are motivated, I was surprised to see that 74 percent are primarily intrinsically driven. They may want to be a master of their craft, to be part of something bigger, or maybe to prove something to someone else or themselves, as Mauricio did.

In addition to the data from OMG, there is a meta-analysis published in the *Journal of Vocational Behavior* by Timothy Judge and colleagues that synthesized 120 years of research and the findings from ninety-two quantitative studies. The analysis reported that intrinsic motivation is a stronger predictor of job performance than extrinsic motivation. The more we focus on money, the less we focus on satisfying curiosity, learning new skills, or having fun, and those are the very things that make us perform at our best.

What the researchers found is that the association between salary and job satisfaction is very weak. The results show that there is less than 2 percent of overlap between pay and job satisfaction levels. These findings align with what I have seen with the sales teams who have come to me for training and coaching: most are primarily intrinsically motivated.

It is important to understand that there are a lot of variables that will impact motivation. It is not all or nothing. For example, it depends on whether the task (or job) you are required to do is interesting to you. If it is boring, for example, intrinsic motivation is less important.

That must be why my grandfather told me to make work fun!

The third type of motivation I measure for is altruistic. Those who are altruistically motivated seek to serve others and help them any way they can, and focus on the welfare of others before their own. Altruistic motivation is what you might call a "servant mindset." More factors are needed to determine how well this motivational style works in sales. It could be that, without their own agenda, they won't be able to move a decision forward. It could also be that the drive to solve a problem for someone, or make the world a better place, means that they will stop at nothing to do so.

Then there are those who are a blended balance of all three styles. Eleven percent of top salespeople are motivated by all three ways.

Understanding your motivational style is key to helping you set personal goals that will shift your mindsets toward sales and change the behaviors and habits that will get you to those goals. As the data shows, money alone is not likely to be enough of a motivator for long-term behavioral change. You will need to dig deeper.

Six months after I started working with Mauricio, he had made his quota and moved off his performance improvement plan. More than that, he went on to sell the largest deals in the company's history and became the top salesperson there for two years in a row.

You know when you see someone accomplish something major, such as writing a book, climbing Mt. Everest, or losing a lot of weight? The first thing you want to know is how they did it, so that you can do it too. Mauricio's manager, David, was amazed at his turnaround and immediately asked me to show him, step by step, how to do the same with the rest of his team. After I worked with David, he was able to help his team consistently hit over their numbers and become one of the top-performing teams in their publicly traded company.

When and if you want to scale your business by hiring new sellers or managers, knowing how—and how much—they are motivated will help you train and develop their skills.

But it took more for Mauricio than understanding his motivational style and his reasons for wanting to prove himself. How and how much you are motivated is one piece to create the incentive to change that will guide you to shift your mindsets, alter your actions, and accomplish your goals.

That's what this chapter is about: I will show you how to feed that fire in your belly and create a system that will nurture your own incentive to change so that you can shoot past your goals, just as Mauricio did, and prove everyone—including yourself—wrong.

You are capable of so much more than you imagine. You only have to give yourself permission to imagine it.

Which brings me to the next motivational myth we need to address.

Motivational Myth Number 2: Magical Thinking

Does "giving yourself permission to imagine success" sound like fluffy "positive thinking"? What's next, am I going to talk about vision boards? Sabbaticals? Maybe you are thinking, "Give me a break—stuff doesn't happen by wishing, it happens by doing. There is no 'secret' to success, it comes with hard work."

If you are thinking that, then, yes, academic research says you are right.

Didn't expect that one, did you? It caught me off guard too, which is why I felt I needed to offer you a disclaimer before we start down the path of finding your ultimate purpose in life. I get it: it's nice to think that if we could tap into our ultimate why, the doing will get easier and more consistent, as if by magic.

And, yes, though I did think vision boards were fluffy, and that positive thinking meditations were a waste of precious time, I tried them because all the popular books told me to, and I was willing to try anything to get better at sales so I could get more clients in.

I dug into the psychology to understand what I was seeing happen with myself and my clients.

Then I came across Kou Murayama, who has been studying human motivation for more than twenty years and now leads the Motivation Science Lab with the aim of achieving an integrative understanding of human motivation. In his 2018 article "The Science of Motivation," he writes, "Despite its obvious importance, empirical research on motivation has been segregated... making it difficult to establish an integrative view on motivation."

Despite the number of experiments Murayama ran to find out whether external rewards or competition influenced motivation, none produced conclusive results.

The bottom line is that there is not enough known about motivation to make scientific judgments about it. The seemingly

Purpose is a journey, not a destination.

obvious fact is that change is a process of learning. And when we are motivated to learn, we learn better and faster, and we retain more of what we learn. (Though, as Murayama points out, there is a lot of nuance to this.)

If there isn't a magic process to tap into your motivation, how do you keep the fire in your belly burning?

While there is no exact science, there are some things you can test out for yourself to see what works for you. Because, like willpower and mindsets, motivation can ebb and flow, and to maintain our motivation over the long term, we need to feed it like a fire on a cold winter's day with supportive beliefs and habits.

Find and Focus On Your Why

Sometimes when my clients are struggling to figure out what is personally meaningful enough to them, I ask, "What would you do if you won the lottery? And why that?" Some say they would pay off everything for themselves and their close family. Others add in paying for future college tuitions for kids. Some want to travel the world and do only the work they truly want to do. If you are familiar with Maslow's hierarchy of needs, you will know that it is very difficult to think inspirationally when you are worried about covering the basics of food and shelter. These questions sometimes help my clients break past the immediate here and now and start to envision a future they want.

Meaning matters. But as Murayama reminds us, there is no proven scientific formula for motivation. Yet we know from our own experiences and observations that, without purpose, it is nearly impossible to have long-lasting motivation.

Over nearly two decades of working with business owners, professional sellers, and leaders, as well as doing this work on myself, there are some strategies I have seen work for me and my clients in terms of helping us clearly see our purpose and source of motivation so we can make long-lasting mindset and behavioral change. When I launched out on my own in the fall of 2007 and started the first version of my business, my goal was to replace my lost salary. I was in survival mode. But I couldn't stay in survival mode when things got harder, because if it was only about survival then I would have accepted the six-figure job as a data analyst with a bank. That wasn't what I wanted; it wasn't what truly motivated me. This wasn't only about making a living. It was about making a difference in my life and in the lives of my family members. I wanted a flexible schedule for my kids so I could spend more time with them: bringing them to school, getting to their games early, doing their homework with them. Yes, I still needed to make money, but my purpose wasn't in the money—it was in what the money I made allowed me to do. At that time, it allowed me to have a flexible schedule. This purpose enabled me to think a certain way about decisions and made what I was doing feel important.

Having a sense of purpose helps to filter the overwhelming amount of information we are bombarded with every minute of the day. With a clear purpose, we can choose how to act on that information.

As William Damon, a Stanford professor and a leading researcher on the development of purpose, once wrote, "Purposeful people look ahead to goals they seek to accomplish over the long haul. The psychological benefits of purpose lie in strengths that forward-looking commitments bring: motivation, energy, achievement, hope, and resilience. Purpose is a prime example of how a person's future aspirations can shape the person's self-development."

Our lives are the choices we make. An active and fulfilling life amounts to the deliberate choices we make. You decided to become a business owner—dare I say, a seller—because of a choice you made: to have a certain life you wanted. You have learned many lessons along the way. Now is the time to reflect on those.

Here are three action items that can help you clarify your purpose and the reason why you do what you do.

Unplug

The first mistake I made as a business owner was not taking time off. For the first twelve years of my business, I didn't take a vacation and typically worked some, if not all, of the weekends that my kids were at their father's house. For two years, I didn't take a single day off. I was on autopilot, addicted to the hustle and grind. I told myself that, because I loved my work, I didn't need to take a break from it.

What was happening was that I was easily distracted, overwhelmed, and burning out.

It was then that a member of one of my mastermind groups, Women Sales Pros, flat-out demanded that I take a vacation, or they wouldn't let me come back (or so they threatened). That struck a chord with me, and I booked a long weekend to go whitewater rafting in northern Maine—where there would be no internet or cell phone coverage. My phone was a paperweight.

For the first day, my anxiety was etched all over my face. "What do you mean I can't check my email, or LinkedIn? What if... (insert any silly scenario here)."

But as I slowly let go of being "connected," I started to be able to hear myself think. The fog of activity was lifted from my brain as I started to see how silly it was to stay glued to my phone and to work all the time. I was missing out on the time I was spending with family and friends because I wasn't truly present. My mind was elsewhere. During that long weekend, when I finally turned my phone off and put it in my suitcase, I felt a level of peace and contentment for the first time in years.

And that is when the panic set in.

The kids are almost grown—soon they will be off doing their own thing. What is my purpose now? I realized that I had been keeping myself so busy because I was avoiding this same big question that every empty nester must face. My life's purpose was raising my kids. Now what?

Here is something to understand about purpose and seeking it: your purpose is not static; in fact, it will change as you go through different phases of life. Which is why these action items I am giving you are important to come back to regularly, or to work into your everyday life.

By stepping back from my work, I was able to face the questions of who I wanted to be and what my purpose was. And while I didn't figure it all out in that one long weekend, I made myself and my husband a promise to take more time off to step back and ask the questions to figure it out. I looked at it as our next great adventure. What this long weekend did for me was make me look for ways to bring the feeling of vacation into my day-to-day. (More on this in chapter 10 when we talk about how to get it all done.) I took the idea of unplugging and built it into my daily routine. I started by stopping the habit of waking up and immediately checking my email from bed (before coffee!). Once I mastered that, I next started to limit the number of times I checked social media during the day (still working on this one...). Most recently, I started taking weekends off for the first time in almost two decades and doing yoga and meditation every morning before I start my workday.

All of this has helped me keep my focus on my why and maintain my own mental health (during a pandemic nonetheless), and it turned something that was a forced grind into a task that I felt grateful to be able to do. It opened space in my head for me to be able to reflect on my purpose.

To start digging into what your current purpose is, take time off. Get away from your home office, your email, your social media accounts, and unplug. Doesn't matter if it's in your own backyard or in an Airbnb nearby. Schedule the time and stick to it.

Reflect

The questions we ask ourselves guide the choices we make. Mark Manson, author of *The Subtle Art of Not Giving a F*ck*, writes that when we are seeking out our life's purpose, what we are asking is, "What do I want to spend my time on that is important?"

When looking to find your current purpose, reflect on your past, present, and hopeful future to help discover it. Here are some reflective questions to ask yourself—or, if you learn by talking out loud with someone, you can use these questions as conversation starters with your loved ones during your time off or away. It starts simply by asking why certain things are important to you. Most people need to ask themselves five to six levels of the question "why" to understand where their motivation comes from. These are examples that can get you thinking and reflecting—don't limit yourself to them.

- **What do you look forward to in your day?** This could be in your personal time or your work time. Is it the quiet time in the morning when you can read, meditate, enjoy a cup of coffee, or have breakfast with your family? Is it the end of the day when you can spend time doing your favorite hobby? For me, I look forward to my early morning yoga sessions outside, or walks in the woods with my dog, or quiet time with my family. And then there are those times when I am working with clients and they have an "aha" moment that changes everything. Or the emails I get from past clients who have reached a goal they once weren't sure was possible. These are the moments that bring me joy, that make me feel like everything is right with the world.

- **Why are those things or moments important to you?** Do you love the outdoors because you were raised camping and hiking? Or maybe you enjoy the peace or excitement those activities give to you. Perhaps the work you do is important because it is something you once struggled with and you don't want anyone else to face the same challenge. Maybe you feel compelled to make a difference in the world or in others' lives so that the world can become a better place.

- **What fires you up?** What makes you so mad that you aren't going to take it anymore? Is it when people are cruel to others whom they see as less than? I become fierce when anyone is cruel to an animal or child. Or when someone gets taken advantage of—for example, scammers going after senior citizens.

- **Ten years from now, what would you want people to say about you?** What would you want your obituary to say? What do you want people to remember about you? Or say about you when you aren't around?

- **What are the best parts of you?** Is it your sense of humor, your grit, your ability to connect the dots, how well you can read and empathize with people?

- **What can you do that no one else can?** Are you able to come up with ideas when others are stumped? Or are you good at seeing the story in the numbers? Perhaps your attention to detail is what makes the difference between a good experience and an incredible one.

- **How do you want to treat others?** Do you want to be the person who lifts others up? Who can always be counted on for a kind word, or a shoulder to cry on?

- **What makes you forget to eat?** What do you get so wrapped up in that time seems to fly by? Psychologists call this "flow": when we are so immersed in something, everything else gets forgotten. This happens for me when I write, or garden, or am in the middle of an engaging coaching call with a client.

When you unplug and reflect on these questions, it may still be difficult for you to answer them. As my colleague Jamie Crosbie says, you have to dig out the "why behind your try."

Journal

When you find yourself stuck, journaling on these reflective questions can help you find your answers.

I know, more writing. Why am I asking you to do so much writing?

When I was growing up, my mother gave me a blank journal every year to write in. I saved them all, and recently went back and scanned through them. I was amazed by some of the things I was so worried about as a kid, but more amazed to see how my thinking changed, and what I learned about myself and the world around me the more I wrote.

When you write, you make new connections in your brain. When you reflect on past experiences and future plans, you form new perspectives and ideas.

Though I don't journal daily as I used to, whenever I find myself at a loss for answers or direction, I pull out a journal and pour everything that runs through my mind into it.

Once it's on paper, it's out of my head. I can look at it more objectively because it is literally in front of me.

This is why I recommend that you write with pen and paper as much as possible. When you do, you can get all those swirling thoughts out of your head and onto paper where you can more clearly examine them. More than this, it helps to calm your mind, similar to meditation. According to a 2010 study by Karin Harman James, associate professor of psychological and brain sciences at Indiana University, writing by hand helps your brain unlock your creativity when it is not easily accessed in any other way. Magnetic resonance imaging showed that analog writing increases activity in the part of our brain that helps us achieve a meditative state.

Use the prompts in the previous section to kick-start your thinking and writing.

Put a Pin in It

Some people spend their entire lives trying to find their purpose, as if purpose were a fixed thing. It seems that the trend to start with "your why" has left many in a frozen state, afraid to take any steps forward without that magical realization. Now the search for purpose has become an excuse for inaction.

Think differently about your purpose—not as something you find, but as something you develop. Research by William Damon, the Stanford University professor I mentioned earlier, suggests that a sense of purpose is driven by action and passion.

You don't think your way into your why, you work your way into it.

Your why is an evolution, not a revelation. To find your purpose, you must do something.

Look at anything in life or nature: nothing stays in the same state. Everything is undergoing constant expansion or contraction. Your purpose is not fixed, it's fluid. It will ebb and flow with your level of self-awareness, the different stages of your life, and the intentions you bring into your day-to-day.

Purpose is a journey, not a destination.

When I ask you to unplug from your regular distractions, reflect on what is important to you, and journal those thoughts, what I am really asking is for you to put a pin in where your purpose lies right now, at this stage of the game. Know that it will change, and that is okay. It is the practice of tuning into your purpose and making it a regular habit that is important. You will need to do this to take the next step in your mindset and behavioral changes so that you can reach the goals you have for your business and life.

The next step is simple, but—as many might say—not so sexy. And that is to set your personally meaningful goals.

Okay, you groaned a little and rolled your eyes when you read that, didn't you? I get it. Goal setting is something everyone tells you that you need to do. You might be thinking that goal setting is a waste of time, because things hardly ever end up happening the way we plan. So, what's the point?

Here's the point: once you have started to get clear on your current purpose, the source of your motivation, you will open yourself up to goals that you might not have realized fully before.

But does goal setting equal motivation? No, the research doesn't back that up. This is why setting the traditional SMART goals (Specific, Measurable, Attainable, Relevant, and Time-based) doesn't always get us there. We make them and forget them.

Does it matter if we set goals? Absolutely, and in so many ways. Yet research is still coming out on the best way to set those goals, and what gets in our way of reaching them.

Behavior change is not an exact science. What we do know is that there are things that make a big difference in how we achieve it. Before I send you down that path, I want to show you some potholes to look out for. Your purpose, your goals, and the changes you want to make to your business and your life are too important to rush through or take lightly.

KEY ACTIONS AND TAKEAWAYS

Even though we must make it #notaboutme to be #buyerfirst, understand that motivation can ebb and flow and we must constantly feed it by being mindful of our own beliefs, values, and reasons why we do the work. This is where you can and should make it all about you. The act of selling is about making a behavior change happen. To make any behavior change happen, we must first understand the motivation that drives us to do so. When we understand the process of why we want to change, it becomes easier to help our buyers do the same.

By developing a process to tap into and feed your motivation, you will have a better understanding of what might drive your buyers to make a behavior change too.

9

SET YOUR GOALS, NOT SOMEONE ELSE'S

The hardest thing about life is knowing what matters and what doesn't... If nothing matters, then there's no point. If everything matters, there's no purpose. The trick is to find firm ground between the two ways of being.

AMY HARMON

EARLIER I SHARED with you that I struggled with weight for most of my life. The first memory I have about being overweight was realizing that when most of my relatives talked about me and my sister, I was the smart one and she was the pretty one.

But the real stinger was cheerleading try-outs. Nine-year-old me thought jumping around, yelling, and dancing with pom-poms would be so much fun.

Oh, the pom-poms—that was all I wanted.

That is what I focused on during one summer vacation as I sat in a middle-school gym that smelled of moldy shoes. I learned how to skip step, sing-song chant loudly, and do a split. I watched in awe as the experienced varsity girls with their perfect ribboned ponytails and their matching socks went through complicated routines without a mistake or a stumble.

I wanted to be them. I wanted to look like them, act like them, and, yes, to smell like them.

After a week of nerves, sweat, and a few awkward falls, it was audition day. "I've got this. I can do this. Just have fun, right?" I repeated this mantra to myself as I sat in the hallway outside the gym, waiting for my pod to go in for the try-outs. I was nauseous. This didn't feel fun at all.

Why was I doing this again?

When our turn was called, the five of us went into the gym and set out in a line. Mrs. G., the head coach, checked her list, called out our names, and asked for the first routine. With sweaty palms, I panicked. What was the first move again? I took the first step and muscle memory took over. I didn't forget anything, didn't fall, and was loud and clear. Although I was taller and bigger than the other girls, I kept in step with them. Phew! They were only going to take six girls out of the twenty-four who were trying out and I had never done this before, but still, I was sure I made the cut.

After every pod had gone in and executed their try-out, we were all called back. One by one, Mrs. G. called out the six chosen names, and mine wasn't one of them. I was disappointed, but not ready to give up yet. Maybe I could try again later.

When all the squealing stopped and people started heading out to the parking lot, I followed Mrs. G. out and asked what I did wrong—what should I work on?

"Oh, nothing honey, come back next year when you lose that baby fat."

What baby fat?

I would never be one of those pretty girls with their perfect ponytails.

As psychologically damaging as that was, I understand now that I had set my goal based on my view of others, and so I was comparing myself to that. If I could be *that*, or look like *that*, I would be happier.

If you could get ten more clients in, or be more like (insert your comparison of the day here), then you will feel successful and things will get easier, right? Like my client Mauricio, who wanted to get off his performance plan and hit over his quota to get into a management role—that was what everyone else around him was doing, after all.

I spent the better part of my adolescent and early adult years looking in the mirror, wishing I was someone else. Everywhere I turned, I saw people I could compare myself to, and I always found myself lacking. Social media is a feeding ground for our inner critics. Comparison is the death of confidence.

I tried weight-loss programs, shake diets that tasted like cake batter, meal plans with exact measurements and specific foods, and exercise plans. Sometimes the weight came off, but nothing kept it off, and I never made it to my goal of becoming a size eight.

How many goal setting planners and programs have you been through? How many New Year's resolutions have you made but not stuck with? I find that when I talk about goal setting with my clients, I either get the same eye roll you did earlier (*This is a waste of time. Can we get started and do what we need to do?*) or the eagerness of a kid in a candy store (*If I dig into my why and purpose, everything will fall into line for me because I have put my intention out into the universe...*)—only to then watch them experience the same type of crash you see when a kid comes down from their sugar high.

Does this mean goal setting doesn't work at all? That we shouldn't bother? Far from it.

Yeah, It Matters

I analyzed the Objective Management Group (OMG) data (again) and it showed that salespeople with personally meaningful goals are 298 percent more likely to reach elite-level performance than those without. The analysis also revealed that salespeople with goals have 32 percent greater abilities than those who don't have them. Abilities such as active listening and asking enough targeted questions, focusing on value over price, and negotiating—everything you have read about in this book. When we have personally meaningful goals, we learn more and perform better!

Personally meaningful goals that are written, shared, and regularly reported on help you develop the keystone habits necessary to make changes in your sales mindsets, behaviors, and results.

Why did I leave this topic for the end of the book? Why didn't we start here? (My editors asked me this same question too.)

Would you have believed me at the start of this book if I had told you that your biggest dreams were possible? That somehow, this time will be different?

Only 45 percent of professional sellers have personally meaningful goals that are written down and tracked for progress. But why? If setting goals is so important to success, why don't we do it?

Allow me to once again call out the elephant in the room by addressing some of the deep psychological reasons we procrastinate goal setting, or fail to reach the goals we do set.

Remember Michael Douglas, from chapter 4? Michael came to me because he wanted to make two or three more sales a year. He felt that was doable. After two months of coaching, he started to see small, quick wins. The nature of his conversations changed, and he began meeting with higher-level executives.

After six months of coaching, he sold more than he had in his previous three years at the company. He never thought it would be possible, and if someone had told him this would happen, he would have laughed in their face.

"Now I know that anything is possible," he told me.

After Michael shared this with me, I couldn't shake one question: How does our outlook—our belief about the future—impact our mindset toward goal setting and learning?

If you think back to Motivational Myth Number 2 in the previous chapter, you'll recall that I once had a hard time buying into the "put it out to the universe" way of thinking. When people accused me of being too negative, I shot back that I was a realist who prepared for the worst because I hate surprises or disappointment. That seemed like the smart thing to do to be more productive and to improve my current circumstances.

But according to Shawn Achor, author of *The Happiness Advantage*, over 200 scientific studies prove that happiness raises nearly every outcome of our lives, from health and quality of life to productivity and—you guessed it—sales.

My own analysis of the OMG data about the impact of our outlook on our ability to learn and grow aligned with Achor's research. Sellers with a strong outlook are 41 percent more motivated, have 25 percent more desire for success, are 45 percent more committed to doing whatever it takes to reach their goals, have a 51 percent higher "Figure It Out" factor (a measure of how quickly we learn), and are 29 percent more likely to have a system to track their goals and progress.

A negative outlook dampens your motivation, desire, commitment, and ability to learn quickly. More than that, it causes you to think small.

Functional MRI findings published in 2007 by Tali Sharot, Alison Riccardi, Candace Raio, and Elizabeth Phelps of New York University and the Wellcome Centre for Human

Neuroimaging at University College London show that optimism activates both the amygdala and a part of our brain called the rostral anterior cingulated cortex (rACC). This helps us downplay negative emotional responses and drives us to go after higher-stakes goals.

The study also showed that an optimistic outlook enables us to learn and understand more easily, and helps us stay focused on near-term events and successes. As Michael's outlook on the future started to change with quick wins, he began to believe that bigger things were possible.

A negative outlook is kryptonite to almost anything we are trying to accomplish. In addition to its impact on our level of motivation, desire, and commitment, its dampening effect on bravery, grit, curiosity, and empathy means you may be bailing out in tough situations, or becoming more emotional than normal. And those tough situations can include anything that seems risky—for example, prospecting (*no one wants to talk to me*), qualifying (*the reason they gave isn't enough for them to change the status quo*), setting goals (*I have to be realistic, what if I fail?*), managing your time (*I have no control over that, too many people need me*), or trying to learn or unlearn a skill or habit (*why bother, AI is going to replace it*).

If you are struggling with sales and you often say things like, "Why me? I can't seem to catch a break!" or "Of course it fell apart, I knew that would happen," it might be time to change your outlook and reframe how you see the future.

But how?

I realized as I was writing this chapter that there was never a point where either Michael or I simply decided to change our outlook. Instead, it happened as we found small examples of success. These quick wins boosted our confidence in our ability to make the changes, and opened us up to what was possible in the future.

If you haven't done the exercises in this book yet, go back and try them. Reading about how others have done it, or how you should do it, is not going to get you there. No one ever won the game by staying on the sidelines. Seek out those small, quick wins to build your confidence and change your own outlook of what the future holds.

What will happen when that crazy daydream I showed you how to feed in the previous chapter comes true? How will life be different for you and everyone around you? Focus on that and write that vision down here.

The crazy daydream I have is...

When this daydream comes true, what will my daily life look like? (Engage all of your senses—what will it look like, sound like, smell like?)

This is important to me because... (How does this align with your values and purpose?)

I will be sharing this with... (Who else is with you in this vision? Family, friends, pets? Or is this for yourself?)

When this happens, I will feel… (Write down the first emotion that comes to mind.)

As an early guess, this is what my income will look like when all this is happening:

Now, how do you change your outlook after a lifetime of disappointments and hard circumstances so that you can set goals that will change your life?

How to Develop and Maintain a Positive Outlook

Look at changing your outlook and your behaviors in the same way as if you were changing your daily eating habits. The more consistently you do it, the more you will see progress, until eventually it becomes an unconscious habit. Some days and situations will be easier than others when you first start. The key is to start and *keep* starting.

Here are three strategies my clients and I have used to develop and maintain a positive outlook.

Don't believe everything you think. Head trash is real. When a negative thought enters your mind, don't ignore it—examine it. What is the most common negative thought you have? When you wrote down your crazy daydream, what was the first doubt that came to your mind? Write it down here:

____

____

Where did that thought come from? Is there any foundation to it? Write that connection down:

____

____

How will that fear or doubt impact you and others around you? Is there anything you can do about it? (You know the drill by now.)

____

____

Accept that it is what it is. Do you, like me, hate that saying? Every time I used to hear it, my immediate thought was, "Yeah—it is what it is because you are accepting the status quo! What a cop-out." But the reality is that accepting where you are now is what will allow you to slow down, examine that situation, change what you can, and move on from the rest. If you can identify an action you can take, then take it. But if you can't, then your only choice is to accept it. To help reframe this thinking, create an "oh well" statement for these situations. For example, your buyer went with your competitor? "Oh well, there are others out there who need my help. I'll see how things go with those buyers in three months." Write down your own first "oh well" statement here:

____

____

Practice daily gratitude. I write in a journal when I am struggling with my outlook or when I need to process a situation. I start with the things I can recall from the day before that were positive. Sometimes the list is long; sometimes I struggle to find one thing. But there is always at least one thing. Even if it's only the fact that today is a new day and a fresh start, or that my husband made it home from his long commute, it's something. Take a moment to reflect on one small thing to be grateful for and write it down here:

____

____

When you start to appreciate where you are now, you may see how much more you are capable of and what a way forward might be. The next thing you need to figure out is how to reach it—what are the steps you need to take, or keep taking? How do you make the changes and not slide back into old habits?

Ditch Cookie Cutters

In chapter 2, I introduced you to Wharton professor Katy Milkman and her book *How to Change*. Milkman shares that for us to alter our behaviors and make it stick, we need a specific strategy that considers our unique strengths and weaknesses—not a quick fix or a general strategy used by others, because they are not us.

Head trash is real. When a negative thought enters your mind, don't ignore it—examine it.

I learned this lesson when my friend Judy, a professional organizer, came over to help me declutter and make sense of the chaos that was my home office. I tended to put all paperwork into a pile to be sorted out later, but later never came. I was losing important documents, or taking far too long to find them, and it was becoming frustrating and time consuming.

I asked her what her process was and what I needed to do.

"There isn't one," she said.

"So how can you help me?" I asked.

Judy explained that it was common for people to get frustrated with her when she couldn't offer a proven process for them to adopt. But, she told me, trying to adopt someone else's organization process would not work over the long term because eventually our habits take over and the mess comes back. Instead, her process is to ask a lot of questions to determine what a given client's tendencies are, and then create a plan that accounts for those default tendencies so it will be easier for them to stick to it.

One frustration for me was losing bills in the mail and then having to pay late fees. She had me walk through how I collect my mail, where I put it, and how I sort it. Turns out, leaving your mail in the car or in a pile on your desk isn't a good system. But for me, I hate bookkeeping and don't want to spend much time on it, so I was dumping it and forgetting it. But the piles and the sorting of the piles had become distracting and stressful.

Judy had me put a mail sorting slot next to the trash can so I could bring in the mail, throw out the junk right away, and then put bills and checks in one mail slot and personal mail in another. I later developed this system into not getting bills at all and having everything on autopay. But to make getting started easier, I needed to make the change smaller so it would be easier to stick to.

The same thing would happen for me with the latest diet or workout program: it never worked over the long term because it didn't consider my individual mindsets, strengths, and weaknesses. I was trying to follow someone else's footprints, but the steps were too wide, the hill too steep, and the path unclear.

This is why the secret that some other business owner once used to make six figures in six months may not work for you. And why the new, trendy sales process or methodology doesn't transform the average success of sellers much above the standing 50 percent range. The best you can hope for from others' success is to learn a thing or two to try out for yourself. But it won't be based on scientific research or data, so you can't repeat it. It is based only on the limited experience of one person.

Do a Confidence Check

Among the many roadblocks I see business owners and sellers bump into on their path to setting goals and reaching them, two of the most common are a lack of confidence and too much confidence. Those who do all those exercises I have described so far—vision boards, meditation, and so on—often let those practices fall by the wayside, like a New Year's resolution that fizzles out. Why do all the tools and techniques to help us set meaningful goals often fail to change our behaviors? Why do most New Year's resolutions fail?

One New Year's Eve, my sister convinced me to do the Whole30 diet with her. If you aren't familiar with this, it is a thirty-day elimination program in which you "reset" your diet. You don't consume grains, legumes, dairy, alcohol, added and artificial sugar, or foods with common additives such as carrageenan, MSG, and sulfites. Not having flour, butter, sugar, or my regular glass of wine was tough. The legumes I could live without.

Networking events were a grueling test of my willpower. There is nothing but booze and cheese plates at every one of them. Eating at home seemed impossible too. There was more than one time when I stood in the grocery store reading labels, feeling so hungry and frustrated that I wanted to scream and cry at the same time. Everything had sugar in it!

By the tenth day, I had such headaches that I almost gave up. But I pushed through with every ounce of willpower I could summon. The creators of the program had explained that this would happen, but said that if you toughed it out, you would eventually start thinking more clearly, sleeping better, and feeling better.

By the third week, I realized they were right. I felt incredible—I wanted to keep doing this forever! I had lost a little weight, become used to the restrictive meals. I could do this!

And yet, sixty days later, I was sitting on an airplane with a slice of pizza in my hand. *I'll get back to the Whole30 program when I'm not traveling, or when it's not the holidays—or when it's not a Thursday.*

My initial overconfidence in my willpower sunk me because I didn't consider the fact that there would be ups and downs in following the Whole30 diet. Have you ever felt this way after reading the latest sales book—you get excited to try it out, and if it doesn't work, or you aren't able to repeat the success right away, you give up? We tend to overestimate our strengths and underestimate our weaknesses, and it's worse when we are inexperienced.

Okay, so a lack of confidence and overconfidence are equally damaging to our ability to set goals and stick to them. What is the right amount of confidence, then?

When you set your goals, make sure you account for all of the obstacles and setbacks you may face, so that you don't give up at the first signs of resistance or failure. Start now by writing down the top three obstacles you have faced in the past when going after your goals.

My top three obstacles are:

1 ______________________________

2 ______________________________

3 ______________________________

When you see one of these come up again, what will do you to remind yourself of your goal? How will you work through it? Write it down now—choose an action or strategy from the ones you wrote down earlier and pick the one you will start with. Just one.

To work through these obstacles, I will:

____

____

Psychologist Albert Bandura has defined confidence, or self-efficacy, as people's belief in their capabilities to exercise control over their own functioning and over events that affect their lives. Our sense of self-efficacy can provide the foundation for motivation, well-being, and personal accomplishment.

Because I had tried and failed to lose the weight so many times, I didn't have confidence that I would ever be able to do it. Most of my family is overweight; it's in our DNA—you can't fight genetics. It didn't matter if I wanted to lose five pounds or fifty. Didn't matter when my doctor told me I was pre-diabetic, my cholesterol and blood pressure were rising, and I was in an elevated danger for heart attack or stroke. I couldn't make myself set a goal and then miss it—again. What was the point? *I feel fine now; this is only because the doctors want to put me on more pills.* (There was that "present bias" working its evil magic on me.)

You see this happen when you hit a slump and it feels as if no matter which way you turn, you are faced with a wall of "no."

Or when you're doing something hard and don't see success fast enough.

When your confidence is low, focus on your past successes, or something that you accomplished before that you once thought impossible. Many times while writing this book, I felt my confidence in my ability to finish bottom out. Writing a book is a lot of work, and juggling it while still serving my clients and running my own business sometimes seemed impossible. And the first draft? Not so good...

That is when I would remind myself that I had felt the same way when I was working two jobs while raising two boys alone and going to college at night full time. That had been a lot of work too, and it didn't always go well, but I did it and managed to graduate at the top of my class. *If I can do that, I can do this too.*

Reflect now for a moment and write down a time when you overcame a challenge or accomplished something new.

When my confidence is low, I will remember when I:

____

____

If that doesn't work for you and your confidence still feels weak, another way to strengthen it is through practice. I shared with you the importance of practice for skill building in chapters 5 and 6, and it is equally critical to your confidence. The more you practice (and improve), the more your belief in your ability to do something will grow. And remember, you can always go back to the quick wins I laid out for you in the earliest chapters of this book. Doing those exercises can help you build confidence in the fact that you can make changes happen, and that those changes will work for you. Write down even the smallest of wins—each one is a building block.

And when you're ready to dig into goal setting in more detail, open up the **Buyer First Workbook** folder, which you have (I hope!) downloaded from **bit.ly/buyerfirstworkbook**, and open the "**Goal Setting Worksheets.**" As Lao Tzu wrote, "The journey of a thousand miles begins with one step." Use these worksheets to reevaluate your goals every year, or however often is right for you. Talk with family and friends about your shared daydreams, or take yourself on a retreat for solo reflection. In the following sections, we will dig deeper into how to make that dream happen, and start to form a plan of action.

Create Your Fresh Start

You might be wondering when is the best time to set your goals. There is no bad time, or specific time that is better than any other. There is no day like today, no time like right now. But there is some evidence that milestones play a part in getting us to make a change and set goals.

In *How to Change*, Katy Milkman shares that her research suggests that we can motivate ourselves to make a change if we look at goal setting as a way to create a fresh start. It is why we still set New Year's resolutions; when we want to change, it helps to have a new beginning, a clean slate—a chance to wipe away the past failures that haunt us. But you don't have to wait until New Year's to get that fresh start. There are plenty of ways to create clean slate opportunities for yourself, such as birthdays and other calendar events, or major life events like buying a house, starting a new job, or starting your own business in a pandemic. Anytime we do something new, that is an opportunity to look ahead from a clean slate.

My forty-fifth birthday was in the fall of 2019, right before the COVID pandemic started. I decided that my birthday present to myself would be that Noom subscription I described earlier. I had seen the ads claiming that the program uses a cognitive behavioral approach to weight loss, to make it stick long term. Since that is what I do with professional sellers every day, I knew what kinds of results it could have, and thought that maybe it would work to apply it to my own struggles with weight loss.

I had a fresh start date: my birthday. I had an inkling of how it would work, and I was hopeful. The ads showed examples of people like me who had lost the weight and kept it off—all of this together gave me a certain level of confidence that it could work.

When my birthday arrived and I began my weight-loss journey with Noom, I was prepared to start fresh, with an open mind that put aside any past failures. *That was then, this is now*, I thought, and I was hopeful that this time would be different. I wanted my energy back, my strength. I didn't want the aches and pains I felt every day, all day. I wanted to keep up with my adult kids and hike the national parks. I wanted to be healthy, not thin. I wanted to feel better as well as look better.

To make your own fresh start, set an intention by giving it a name. Milkman found that labeling the change influences both how we act and how we describe ourselves. Healthy Carole would do things differently.

Open your calendar right now. Do you have a big date coming up? A birthday? A class or family reunion that you can go to and share your successes with? If you don't, that's okay. Monday mornings are a fresh start opportunity that happen every week. In fact, every new day is a fresh start, if you think about it. Set a date with yourself for when you will think about the daydream you wrote down earlier, or when you will talk about it with your significant other. As you think and talk, consider when you want to reach that goal, what kind of first milestone you can set on your path, and on what date you will reach that early milestone.

When you pick a date on the calendar, you are taking the first step to creating your fresh start. But this is only the beginning.

Here are a few more steps that you will need to take to set the type of personally meaningful goals that will drive you to do more.

Make the Commitment

Do you know why they call marriage a commitment? It is in writing, declared publicly to others, and there are consequences (and rewards) if you do or don't do the things you made a vow to do. In terms of your sales growth, commitment takes the form of how willing you are to do whatever it takes (ethically) to get to your goals.

How you make that commitment is similar to how you commit to a marriage. To make a commitment to something, first you must define it—which is what all that thinking, talking, and envisioning the future was about. The next step is to write those goals down. It can be a digital document, or pen and paper, but it's only a thought or a dream until you can produce a document stating your goal. Writing it down makes it real.

Write down your goals with a deadline you want to have them happen by and a dollar amount you need have set aside to make it happen—because taking time off work will require a certain amount of money in the bank to keep the bills paid. Another thing you will need is a definition of what "being the best" or "proving it" looks like: How will you know when that has happened? What will you be able to point to and say, "I did it"?

When I decided to go on my Noom weight-loss journey, I knew I would need to be able to see that I was making progress. What number do I need to hit to be considered healthy? Is the scale going down? Is my waist getting smaller? Am I sleeping better? Can I walk farther in the same amount of time? These were all measurable indicators that could tell me I was getting healthier.

How will you track your progress? Is it the number of email responses you get? The number of sales meetings on your calendar? The movement of the opportunities in your CRM? Identify

Success breeds confidence, so set up small wins for yourself to build up that confidence over time.

what you need to track to know you are making progress. You may have different places for your data, in which case tools such as Databox can help you put your metrics all in one place with simple dashboards and compare your metrics to others like you. Compare your sales metrics with other business owners who sell here: bit.ly/salesbenchmark.

Break It Down

If I never had those goals written down, it would have been impossible for me to know if I was making progress. To know what progress is, I needed to do the next step in committing to my goals—which is to create an action plan that breaks down those goals into small steps, or into habits that need to be developed.

When you break down your goal into manageable pieces, it takes some of the anxiety out because you don't need to keep thinking about it. Each piece builds on the commitment you are making to yourself.

Another benefit to breaking down your big goal into smaller goals is that each small goal you reach increases your confidence. Success breeds confidence, so set up small wins for yourself to build up that confidence over time. Because you are focused on the smaller goal and behavior, the larger change is more reachable and less overwhelming.

When I did the math to calculate what my healthy weight and BMI would be, the idea of losing seventy-five pounds felt overwhelming. I hadn't weighed that little since my senior year of high school! It seemed an impossible goal. Was it possible?

I felt the same sense of hopelessness as I did when I was in labor with my first son. He was a big boy at eleven pounds and two ounces. I remember staring at the clock, pushing, waiting for that one minute to be up when I could rest. *This kid is too big—I can't do it!* I don't know where the thought came from, but I remember thinking to myself that women have been doing this—delivering babies—for thousands of years. And all without doctors, hospitals, or pain medication. *If they can do it, I can do it.*

When I set my new healthy weight goal, I reminded myself of that moment. Here I was again, faced with something that felt impossible, that I didn't feel confident I could do. But by recalling how I had once successfully done something that seemed equally impossible, I gave my confidence a boost and I became willing to try.

The same thing will happen to you when you write down your goals. If they relate to more clients and more money than you have ever reached before, that might scare you a bit, and that is a good sign. The bigger the goal, the bigger the challenge, the bigger the change you will go through.

That's why it's important to stick to one goal at a time, no matter how big or small it is. Maybe your goal wouldn't be that big to someone else, but to you it is. In the "**Goal Setting Worksheets**" in the **Buyer First Workbook** (**bit.ly/buyerfirst workbook**), you will see that you are never asked to write down more than three goals in one plan. This is designed to save your sanity and to set you up to be able to prioritize your time later, which we will talk more about soon.

No matter how big and scary your goals may or may not be, the next step in committing to them is to break down your ultimate goal into micro goals. You started the work on your milestones in the previous section, and now this is the time to really lay out that plan. The question to ask yourself is this: "What are the smaller milestones that, once achieved, get me closer to my ultimate goal?"

Your action plan will be a work in progress, in the same way that you are a work in progress. As you shift your sales mindsets and develop the necessary skill sets, you will discover other areas where you want to improve because of the impact it has on your circumstances now. When that happens, write it down in your action plan with the impact you are seeing and the strategy you are going to try to practice in order to overcome those areas. You may find as you work toward your goals that more things come up that you need to overcome. That is to be expected. A growth mindset is one that is looking for consistent improvement. When one thing is mastered and becomes a habit, it is time to focus on the next challenge.

The aim is to have a goal with specific behaviors and actions you want to learn and apply so that you can take the next step to committing to—or marrying—your goals. For many people, this next step is the scariest part: declaring your goal and action commitments to someone else.

Yes, that's right. By the end of your goal setting exercise, you should be able to come up with a goal declaration statement that you will make to another person. It will be something that sounds like this:

> My goal for next year is <insert your measurable goal here>. This is important to me because it enables me to [be, have, do] <insert your value here>. In order to achieve that goal, I need to work on my ability to <insert area of improvement, or obstacle to overcome>. My strategy to overcome that is <insert action> when <insert cue>. Where I need help is <insert area of improvement> and would appreciate feedback on <insert specific feedback request>.

When I tell my coaching clients that the next step in goal setting is to share their goals and plans with others using this statement, many end up saying to me, "What if it doesn't happen and everyone knows that I failed? I couldn't take the pity looks and embarrassment."

And that is exactly the point.

Out Yourself to Others

To make a further commitment to your behavioral changes—in sales or in any other part of life—once you determine what must be changed and the smaller steps to get to your goal, it's time declare it publicly. According to Milkman's research, the act of public declaration is a soft commitment device. When you don't do what you've said you'll do, it creates cognitive dissonance, or a feeling of being at odds with yourself. You shared your plans with others; now, if you don't follow through, it will haunt you.

When we take extreme responsibility for our outcomes, we can change our circumstances. When we don't, we make excuses and become a victim of our circumstances.

Owning your own business or building your book of business as a seller working remotely is going to feel isolating. When I went from corporate to self-employed, I didn't anticipate how much that isolation would impact me. Other than my kids and husband, I didn't have anyone to bounce ideas off of, practice with, or vent to when I was frustrated and needed to get it out of my system.

What I didn't realize is that what I was craving was some accountability. I needed a way to take ownership of my outcomes. It felt as if my dream of controlling my day, never mind my destiny, was turning out to be anything but. Everything seemed out of control. For me to take ownership of my outcomes and my goals, I needed to "out" myself to others, and tell them my goals and plans to get there.

When I started my Noom weight-loss journey, I knew from my work with sellers and business owners that to make a change I needed a goal, and to commit to that goal, I needed to write it down. (It was rather validating when the Noom app used some of the same research I used with my clients.) When I learned that breaking my goal down into smaller, repeatable changes would make it easier to ease myself into those changes,

I thought that everything would be a piece of cake from there (pun intended!).

Once I had set my goals and plans in the Noom weight-loss app, they matched me up with a virtual coach and put me in a group of other "Noomers" who were starting out as well. Throughout the week, the app sent me educational articles and ideas for strategies on how to incorporate the tactics in my day-to-day. At the end of each exercise, the app prompted me to share my takeaway and action item in the group with my coach, or with someone else.

Yes, at first it felt silly. One exercise that I rolled my eyes at was mindful eating. I learned through the articles and research the app shared that when we eat in front of the TV, or phone, or computer, our brains aren't registering what and how much we are eating. We zone out and end up eating more and faster than we think we are. As a result, we don't feel full until we are overfull—because we ate so much so fast. This small thing was actually a big thing for me. I had learned to eat fast while working in restaurants all through high school and college. You ate when you could, as fast as you could. The habit carried through when I started working from home and would watch TV or have my laptop open as I ate without thought.

I declared this to the group and shared my strategy to start my day by turning all my devices off before I ate breakfast, facing my lake view as I ate instead of looking at a screen. I added that I would have a sip of water between each bite so that it would take twenty minutes instead of ten to finish the meal. I was surprised when other members of the group commented on my post to say that they struggled with the same thing for similar reasons. One person said they traveled a lot, so eating on the run was natural to them. Others had young kids and felt lucky to have time to shower, never mind sit down and eat. I wasn't the only one who had this problem!

Better yet, those who shared their experience also shared what they were trying and how it was working for them. One person commented that, to slow down, they counted ten Mississippis in between bites. Another shared that they put their fork down between bites and put their hands in their lap to slow themselves down. After reading these comments, I felt more confident that the weight loss was something I could do, and I incorporated these other tactics that I hadn't thought of. That week, I broke through a weeks-long weight-loss plateau.

In *How to Change*, Milkman tells us that having an accountability group that gives you advice, and enables you to give your advice, helps you build confidence in your abilities and the changes you want to make. Beyond the "fake it till you make it," by giving advice to others, you become more likely to follow your own advice.

Teach to Learn

In her research, Milkman studied how mentoring others can help the mentor make a behavioral change, because it encourages them to "follow their own advice." This is another way that cognitive dissonance works in our favor: if we tell someone else to do something, we feel compelled to practice what we preach. Milkman calls this the "saying is believing" effect. My grandfather would have said, "What's good for the goose is good for the gander."

Psychologists call this the protégé effect. We make more effort to learn if we expect to teach it to someone else. The impact on your motivation to learn and the mechanics of the learning itself is greater when teaching and mentoring involves asking and answering questions, according to research from Keiichi Kobayashi, a professor of education at Shizuoka University in Japan.

I see this happen with my coaching clients in group sessions. When one individual is struggling in an area, and I know someone else in the group is as well, or is barely getting through it, I ask one of them to give advice to the other: "What would you do if you were them?" And, of course, some reply with, "I don't know—I am struggling with this too!" What they don't know is that this is exactly why I asked them: because they are struggling with it too. However, because it is not them and their sale at stake, it is easier to be more objective. Which is just what I tell them: "That is why you are the best person to give them advice: you know what it is like to be in their shoes. And because this isn't your deal, you have nothing to lose. Since you have nothing to lose, what would you do?"

I swear, sometimes I see light bulbs come on when they realize that, in their own sales conversations, they have nothing to lose because they don't have the deal yet.

I have found this works for me too. When I am training or coaching someone else to prospect more, for example, it compels me to do more of the same. What's good for the goose is good for the gander, after all.

If you aren't able or willing to do this, apply the advice to yourself. If this were a friend struggling, what advice would you give them?

When there are times I am struggling in my own sales process, I listen to my calls and pretend I am the coach, not the person on the call. How would I advise them to adjust their approach or follow-up?

Accountability groups, mastermind groups, and coaching groups are all great ways to practice, build your confidence, and get fresh perspectives on your challenges. It is important to seek out people who have knowledge of your problem that you may have overlooked. We often assume people know what we know, and don't know what we don't know. According to Katie Mehr, Katy Milkman, and several of their co-researchers at Wharton, when we have a group that keeps us accountable, we can copy their strategies and processes, as I did with my Noom group when I shared my plan to eat more mindfully. Seeing what others similar to us do to be successful boosts our own confidence that we can do it too. By seeking it out ourselves, it becomes easier for us to adapt it to fit our style and accelerate our own learning.

Find Your Support Group

Sara was a new sales manager who had come to one of my talks and heard me share that one way to scale one-to-one coaching is to hold group coaching calls of four to five people, in which each person gets ten to fifteen minutes of one-to-one coaching while everyone else listens in. I call it group therapy for salespeople, and it has multiple benefits.

First, it forces transparency. Joining a group and sharing how you messed up or how you are not perfect might seem intimidating. And that is part of the benefit. If you can get over your hang-ups and share with a group, and then hear how others struggle with the same thing, it doesn't seem so bad when you are face-to-face or on the phone with a prospect.

Second, getting multiple perspectives on a problem makes you more accountable to changing your own process and to doing something different. When you get on the next group call and tell everyone about your success or flop, you have a sounding board that can help set you on a better path next time—and, at the same time, you are giving others information on why something did or didn't work.

Third—though perhaps this should be first—it gives the people who are listening in the ability to gain some emotional distance from their own challenges and struggles. To some degree, everyone on the call has an opportunity to "coach" someone else (when guided by the more experienced leader). Because the others are not emotionally involved in the sale, they are able to think outside the box on how to engage. When you are not emotionally involved in a sale, you can see what is happening and offer a different perspective. That in turn helps you reflect on your own situation with less emotional eyes. This falls in line with Milkman's research on how giving advice to others helps us follow that same advice.

Finally, having a group helps you feel as if you are not alone in this. Hearing the challenges that others face in sales situations can be a relief. You can see that others have been there, and have made it to the other side.

Sara loved all these ideas. She went back to her team, divided them up, and launched coaching calls with each group. But after her first few calls, she found that her more experienced sellers were acting like they were a waste of time, and her less experienced sellers were quiet and not participating. Why wasn't this working for her and her team? What was going on?

In her book, Milkman lists a few things to be aware of that can make these group calls a help or a hindrance in terms of making and maintaining behavioral change.

First, choose a group of people who are not far apart from where you are, so you don't get discouraged or frustrated. This is what I learned was happening with Sara's team. She had placed newer sellers with veteran sellers, thinking that one would learn from the other. But what happened was that her veteran sellers were hearing the same unhelpful things over and over, and the newer sellers were intimated by the gap in skill set between themselves and the veteran sellers.

Another important thing to consider when joining any group is the laws of social influence, which state that who we surround ourselves with is important when we are trying to achieve big goals. This can be observed in the old saying, "As goes the manager, so goes the team."

Remember how, in chapter 2, I told you that my analysis of OMG data showed that when managers have certain non-supportive beliefs about sales, their team is 355 percent more likely to hold the same beliefs? Then you'll also remember that the analysis showed that when managers have positive, supportive beliefs related to sales, their team is 1,000 percent more likely to hold those same beliefs. The people you are closest to—the ones you spend the most time with—will impact your beliefs and mindsets and therefore your ability to reach your goals.

There are several ways you can apply this in your day-to-day. You could form a club with other self-employed business owners in your community. You could join a networking and referral group. You could find a sales coaching program for business owners. And there is the Buyer First Community on Facebook as a group for sales professionals and business owners to meet and connect with other like-minded people.

You could also build your support system for accountability, feedback, and moral support with those closest to you who have a vested interest in your success, as well as with those who are more objective. You get to decide who you get feedback from, and what feedback you need from them.

Success is not an island in the ocean you get to by paddling alone. You won't accomplish your goals all by yourself. To reach your dreams, you need to create your own support system, one that can take you outside of your comfort zone and hold you accountable for your behavioral change. Everyone needs a coach. The best of the best use coaching to keep them on track. It's not all about the work, though. If you are reading this and thinking this sounds hard and dreary, then read on—because it doesn't have to be.

For behavioral change to stick long term, you need to be flexible in your strategies, be self-aware of your areas of improvement and their impact, track your behaviors, and maintain a positive outlook.

You've got this. Go back and do the exercises. Keep doing the work.

Reevaluate Regularly

Goal setting is important—and not once, but continuously. This is true not because goals motivate us, but because they lay out a path for us to form habits around. We are more open to learning new things, to failing and trying again, when we are going after a goal that is personally meaningful to us.

Our outlook on the future is a big reason why we set goals—or don't. You can change your outlook as you build your confidence with small, quick wins and through developing your own process for behavior change.

Start by setting a date and time to have the conversation with your loved ones about your goals. Daydream out loud with them about what you would do if anything were possible. Fill out your first version of the Goal Setting Worksheets. Share that with others and hold yourself accountable.

If you want some extra accountability, share your goals with me on social media. Tag me on Instagram (@carolemahoney) and use the hashtag #buyerfirst.

Now, how do you bring all this together to repeat success and learn from failures? How will you track your progress to build your confidence and skills?

KEY ACTIONS AND TAKEAWAYS

Comparison is the thief of your confidence and your positive outlook—both of which are critical for behavioral change. Chasing someone else's dream will only lead to frustration and disappointment. There is no right or wrong way to set your goals, only your way.

Rather than trying to adopt someone else's process to set goals, customize your process according to your own strengths and tendencies. Celebrate your small and big wins, reevaluate your goals regularly, and adjust accordingly. Leverage the concept of a fresh start at every opportunity to help maintain a positive outlook.

Please share your daydream goals with me on social media using the #buyerfirst hashtag. There is nothing that is out of reach for you.

I can't wait to see what you do.

10

STOP CHASING SHINY BALLS

Man plans, and God laughs.

YIDDISH ADAGE

SIX MONTHS AFTER I started my first business, I wrote my first big check to go to New York City for an analytics training and certification course through an enterprise web analytics platform. It was used by top e-commerce brands, which meant I was playing with the big boys now!

Yet I had no enterprise clients, and certainly no e-commerce clients. How could I? I had just landed my first client! No one had asked for this type of work from me. But it was cutting-edge technology and would be the biggest thing to happen to shopping since Amazon started selling books online. I would be one of the first to know how to do it!

Instead, the only thing I accomplished was to drain my meager savings. I had fallen victim to my entrepreneurial ADHD and chased the next shiny and exciting ball. It did not align with where I was and what the next steps toward my goals were.

Holger Patzelt, a professor with the Entrepreneurship Research Institute at the Technical University of Munich, noticed that some symptoms of ADHD resemble behaviors commonly associated with entrepreneurship. As entrepreneurs, we are daring, brilliant, and can see the big picture—which makes us uniquely susceptible to the constant distraction of the next shiny thing. Which makes process and habits all that much more important to keep us in check.

Liz Heiman works with entrepreneurs and business owners to help them create strategies and processes to scale their business. If you study sales, you may recognize her name from the sales training company Miller Heiman. The Miller Heiman Blue Sheet was first created in the 1970s and is one of the first documented processes for understanding and navigating buying and selling habits—with it, the sales profession began to incorporate scientific knowledge. Before this tool came along, sellers assumed they knew what buyers wanted, and simply pushed that solution.

Well, many still do. How you sell matters more than what you sell.

Heiman explained that *process* is the defined steps you take that can be measured, *methodology* is what you do in each step, and *strategy* is how you move from one step to the next. They are different yet connected. I want you to start with your buyer's process so that it can inform your methodology and strategy. As you have been doing the exercises in the Buyer First Workbook, you have started to define the steps and what needs to be done in each one, and you are learning what works to move from one step to the next.

The absence of a documented process makes it impossible to repeat success or experiment to get to success. If you do get new business, you may not know how you did it, which means you won't know how to replicate that success. Or, when you have clients you wish you hadn't taken on, how will you know what happened to make the relationship go sour, or how to avoid such clients in the future?

When you document your process continuously, you will start to see trends and patterns that you can use to create new offerings that align with the current environment. This will reduce your stress and anxiety about what to do to grow your business, and it will give you a path forward during uncertainty.

I hope that you will see this as a way to build experiments within your business—and with yourself. That is what we have been talking about this whole time, isn't it? You have observed some things that made you wonder, "Why does that keep happening? How do I change it?" Once you ask these questions, you can come up with some ideas on the answer.

Now, test your hypothesis out, and when it works you will know why. When it doesn't, you will have an idea of what to test the next time.

That is the scientific process at work. Observe, ask, measure, test, repeat.

So, what are the most important things to document, test, refine, and repeat? If your answer is "my buyers!"... gold star for you.

Not Everyone Is Your Buyer

When I started my marketing consulting practice, I was told to add a 10 percent PITA factor into my invoices. Confused, I wondered why I would need to add flatbread to my offering. Was this some secret I didn't know about?

I learned quickly that PITA stood for Pain-In-The-Ass and that these types of clients should be charged more for the hassle and headaches they cause. Well, forget that—why would I work with people who were such a nuisance I would have to charge them more? Why take those clients on to begin with?

But when I found myself with not one but several clients who made me dread crawling out of bed for a call, I almost gave up on the idea of running my own business.

Instead of talking with my kids about their day when I picked them up, I was using hand gestures to communicate while I talked on my Bluetooth headset to handle the latest urgent client crisis/emergency/opportunity. Rather than helping my kids with homework and having family time, I was shut away in my office, analyzing the data on an Excel spreadsheet or writing the latest campaign that wasn't included in the original scope of work and that I wouldn't get paid for.

The life I had "designed" for myself was making me and my family miserable and poor.

Of course, I wanted new clients who valued my expertise, paid me more, and followed my advice to get results for themselves. But because I was so busy handling my current workload, I didn't have the time or energy to find them.

What I haven't told you yet is that when I did the work that I have laid out for you in this book, my goal was to be able to fire those clients and get new ones. I wanted to enjoy my work again and look forward to talking to my clients every week.

Nine months after I started the work to shift my mindsets and interactions with my buyers, I sent back a payment from one of my biggest PITA clients and told them I was taking my business in a new direction. I fully expected them to be angry and rant at me. When they called me and begged me not to drop them, telling me they would take the increased rate and be more responsive, I looked at the phone in awe. *Well, maybe I am that awesome and they can't bear to part with me? I have been doing great work for them; it's about time they realized it! I simply had to push them a bit to get there.* I agreed—and, a month later, it was back to the same behaviors.

I had wanted to believe they would change, and that I had been the one to get them to change. This, despite that fact that they had provided no evidence they would do so, or commitment they would agree to if they didn't.

What I learned was that, as salespeople and business owners who sell, we never think a relationship with a new client will end up like this. And when we see the warning signs, it is tempting to convince ourselves that we can change them, or that this could be a great opportunity... someday. Just as every girlfriend of mine has said to me about their mate at some point. We have all done it: you think you will be the one to change the way your buyer (girlfriend, boyfriend, spouse, or friend) behaves, and then you explain away the behaviors when they get worse, not better.

What are some of the signs that your prospect or client has bad boyfriend potential? Here are my top five:

1 **They show up late, or not at all, for your dates (aka your meetings).** This might seem harmless enough—we are all busy, right? The reality is that they don't value your time. If they don't value your time now, be assured that they won't value it any more later on, even though they are paying you for it. Count on many missed meetings, or meetings that run well over their allotted time.

2 **They don't pay attention to you.** If a prospect talks over you, or talks for you, they may think that they are the smartest person in the room. If they are checking their email or phone during your meetings, then whatever you are saying is not that important to them. Know-it-all prospects will become clients who question everything you say, or completely ignore your advice. It doesn't matter if you are the expert they hired—they "can learn the same things from a book." (If they could do it for themselves, what has stopped them from doing so?)

3. **They have a wandering eye.** The prospect who thinks that the grass is greener somewhere else is going to be consistently comparing you to others. Nothing you do will be good enough and you will always be on the defense with them. Progress will be stalled because you will be too busy justifying and defending your advice against the latest shiny distraction that has caught their attention.

4. **They insist on "going Dutch."** If a prospect wants to negotiate every line item in your proposal, they might be cheap. Or you might have jumped into a proposal too soon before you had built momentum, buy-in, and trusted advisor status. (This happens to a *lot* of sellers and business owners.) If it is the former, and not the latter, plan on your invoices getting questioned and paid late every time.

5. **They won't introduce you to their friends or family.** One question I will test prospects with is this: "If we do this, and you are happy with the results, are you the person who will tell everyone you know, or are you more likely to want to keep me as your secret weapon?" Your best prospects are most likely to come from your best clients. Referrals and word-of-mouth still trump all other forms of marketing. If someone won't introduce you to their friends and family, wouldn't that send up a red flag? Either they are insecure, or they're ashamed of you.

Of course, hindsight is 20/20. It is not until you realize that you are dreading talking to that prospect or client that you know you have a PITA. What should you do? Break the cycle!

What often happened with me, and what I found was happening with my business owner clients as well, was that we were so focused on getting a customer, any customer, that we never stopped to consider if it was the right one for us. Not everyone can, or should, be your client or customer. Bad-fit clients are a death sentence for any business owner or salesperson. They will use up all of your time (or your coworkers' time), without any progress made toward a decision or result.

That is one extreme end of the spectrum: where anyone is your customer, and you are doing anything and everything to get that next one. It is a sure-fire recipe for burnout. But the other end of the spectrum is where you spend all your time in your cave perfecting your sales process and product, locked away from everything, trying to figure it out as you move from one rabbit hole to the next. Those that make the mistake of always planning and never starting often end up distracted or off course, following after the latest trends and technology, which results in never getting closer to your buyer and goals. It's merely an endless chase after the next shiny bouncing ball. Exciting, exhausting, and often fruitless.

What is the balance between these two extremes? How do you plan enough to know where you are going and what you need to do, without being distracted by every possible thing you *could* do?

The good news is that if you have been doing the exercises in the Buyer First Workbook, you have started your documented plan. As you continue to have conversations with buyers, keep updating those worksheets. Edit the worksheets so that they work for you.

Collaborating with your buyer and creating your plan doesn't start after you have figured everything out. It starts from the moment you think you have an idea to solve a problem. And it doesn't involve a complicated strategy or process to start that collaboration—instead, it involves curiosity.

Once you have done your first iteration of collaboration, summarize your new insights into a buyer persona profile that you can reference and update in the future.

Building Your Buyer

Have you ever been to a Build-A-Bear toy store? My kids called it the salad bar of stuffed animals. They would go into the store and pick out the type of stuffing they wanted inside—firm or soft or somewhere in between—then the fur color, the type of eyes, what shape for a nose, which style of ribbon, and not to mention the bear accessories. They got to pick whatever they wanted in their ideal bear. Documenting your ideal customer profile works in a similar way. With this first layer of research, you have all sorts of parts you can choose from to build out your profile.

But be careful, or it may end up as a scene from the '80s movie *Weird Science*. In the film, classic nerds Gary and Wyatt are humiliated by senior jocks for swooning over their cheerleader girlfriends. Feeling rejected and disappointed and wanting more out of their direction in life, good-time Gary convinces uptight Wyatt that they need a boost of popularity. Over the weekend, Gary uses Wyatt's computer to create a virtual woman with everything they can dream up. Of course, the virtual woman becomes real and wreaks chaos and havoc in their world.

It is easy to make a lot of assumptions about our buyers, much like Gary and Wyatt did of their virtual woman come to life. Starting with a basic understanding of your buyer and then having conversations that bring deeper context is key. But beware again—far too many business owners and marketers spend hours, days, and weeks agonizing over every detail of their ideal customer profile or buyer persona. It's impossible to know everything, and not everything is important anyway. Your buyers are evolving humans—nothing stays the same for long.

This doesn't mean you don't need to document; otherwise, how will you know where you have been and what has changed?

It’s impossible to know everything, and not everything is important anyway. Your buyers are evolving humans—nothing stays the same for long.

Developing your ideal customer profile will be an evolution. Let's dig into how to start to build a buyer profile without getting too caught up in the weeds and letting procrastination find a foothold.

In the **Buyer First Workbook (bit.ly/buyerfirstworkbook)**, you will find the "**Buyer Persona Workbook Template**," which you can use for yourself—again and again. (Make sure to save a blank copy!)

The first step is the demographic and background information as well as the event triggers that can be found with the low-touch research you did through your social media and internet searches in chapter 5.

The remaining information comes from the combination of your low-touch research and the conversations you have with your suspected buyers and/or those in your referral list who know the people in the roles you want to work with. Their mannerisms, communication style, beliefs, and motivations are all pieces of information you can learn from high-touch conversations.

Your understanding of their goals and challenges is another form of information that is best learned through direct conversation. This is where you can document the questions you hear them ask most often—in conversations, forums, or comments they make on social media.

Once documented, this information is then easier to update and iterate. Mark on your calendar when you will do so next. Your buyer persona profiles, process, and strategy will evolve over time, as will you and your business.

Which brings us to the next important information for you to document: your own behaviors.

Get Stuff Done

You have learned why personally meaningful goals are important to your sales success, and that by writing them down, sharing them with others to make yourself accountable, and committing to an action plan you are more likely to reach those goals.

To make that plan truly actionable, you will need to detail how and when you will carry out your actions. With what researchers call a "cue-based plan," you will be able to reduce the stress and anxiety common in sales. It is out of your head, no longer a nagging thought that distracts you; now, you can have some thinking room. Doing this type of planning takes some effort and work, and research shows that this will lodge it deeper into our memories.

And you can start it right now. Here are the questions to ask yourself.

What Does Today Look Like?

Write down everything you think you need to do today in a list. If you need more room, find yourself an empty notebook and piece of paper.

My to-do list:

____

____

____

This brain dump is to clear out the clutter in your mind. Next, choose three things that need to get done but that aren't fun. For me, that includes paperwork, anything bookkeeping related, or sitting on the phone for customer support or service. To use a gardening metaphor, these are the weeds that must be pulled. They are tedious, but if you skip them you'll have problems.

My weeds:

1 ______________________________

2 ______________________________

3 ______________________________

Now, from that first "brain dump" to-do list, choose three things that are the seeds—these are the things that will lead to growth and your goal. For me, this is typically where I list my best sales opportunities or marketing campaigns.

My seeds:

1 ______________________________

2 ______________________________

3 ______________________________

Now look at your schedule today. Where in that schedule can you move forward on one of the items you wrote down in your weeds list and one of the items in your seeds list that are important and urgent? If there is room for more, great. If not, move it to the next day's list. Include the details of who it involves, what needs to be done or said, and how you will do it. And remember: goals and plans to reach them should be both written and shared. Share your action plan for today with an accountability partner.

Do all of this again tomorrow. And the day after. And...

What Needs to Happen This Week?

Now you can use a similar format for your weekly plan. Don't do this weeks in advance—plan one week at a time. I use a notebook for my planning and the start of each week is a new page, with a sticky note to mark it.

First, map out the week's milestones. What day are slides due for a presentation, or a big sales meeting, or the PTA meeting? Write down the milestones you have for this week here.

My milestones for this week:

____

____

____

____

____

____

____

____

____

Now look at your calendar for the week. Break the milestones you have listed into time blocks in the week so that, if all else fails, you know the most important thing that needs to get done on any given morning or afternoon.

On another page, brain dump all of your to-dos for the week: who you need to talk to, content ideas, admin tasks, spring cleaning projects—all of it. This will further clear your mind of distractions. Write your to-dos for this week here.

My to-do list for this week:

____

____

____

____

____

____

Now choose your top three most important tasks. Only three! Not everything is important and urgent.

My top three tasks this week:

1 ______________________________________

2 ______________________________________

3 ______________________________________

Last, but not least, what are you looking forward to this week? Where is the fun? This could be time with your family, exploring a new restaurant, visiting a park or museum, or seeing the latest movie. Give yourself something to look forward to and write it down in gratitude.

This week, I am most looking forward to:

____

You can replicate this format to be done monthly and quarterly. First, brain dump everything out in writing, then choose the top three, then create a cue-based action plan by assigning each one a day and time, along with details about what needs to be done.

When I first started doing this, I saw my sales go up 20 percent in six months, simply because less fell through the cracks, I was less stressed and anxious, and I knew what I could say yes to and when to say no to things when they didn't align with my goals. It helped to temper my entrepreneurial ADHD.

While this daily, weekly, and monthly routine can keep you focused and help to break down your actions into small chunks, you still need to make sure you are moving toward your ultimate goal. Reviewing your activities and metrics on a quarterly basis is how you will track your progress.

How Are You Progressing toward Your Goal?

To track your progress, break your annual goal into quarterly milestones. This includes the numbers, assets, actions, and disciplines you need to do and have to get there. With that, begin your quarterly plan by looking at where you are starting from. What is the gap?

Next, reflect on what you have learned in the last quarter. This might be related to a personal discipline. For example, I learned that if I watch TV past 9:30 p.m., I won't be able to get to sleep by 10:30 so I can get up early. I also learned that while we don't do a lot of presentation-style training for clients, it is something that is integrated into our process.

After realizing what you have learned, ask yourself these questions:

- What have I done differently, or what do I need to do differently?
- What is working well, and what isn't?

Finally, look back to see where the fun is in the work. What success can and should be celebrated?

As you do this review, remember to cut yourself some slack. We all have things we plan to do in a day but may not get to, and we all sometimes fail when we try to do new things. When that happens, we can beat ourselves up and give up. Defeatism, or all-or-nothing thinking, erodes confidence. Adopting a growth mindset—that our skills and abilities are not fixed but fluid—will give you the confidence to get going and keep going. Failure is a learning curve. Also, make allowances for emergencies, and offer mulligans for mistakes. Life happens. This way your self-confidence can survive the setbacks and plateaus that are sure to happen.

Tracking your progress toward your goals increases your chances of changing the behavior, building the habit, and bolstering your self-confidence. Tracking helps you avoid forgetting, and helps you keep up the efforts to change until it becomes second nature. You can celebrate success and learn from failures when you track them.

In a world that is designed to distract, and with a brain that is wired to seek safety and pleasure, try to eliminate distractions that take you away from your best work. Turn off your Slack, social, and email notifications. Set specific times in the day when you will check email and other notifications, but otherwise leave them off. Work-life balance doesn't come from clear separation—one will always impact the other. It is more about how you integrate the two, not about how much time you spend in one area or the other.

Start Selling *with* Your Buyers

It is time for the rubber to meet the road. As you've seen in this final chapter, to keep your entrepreneurial ADHD in check, you will need to document your processes and create the systems to track your progress toward your goals, and to stop yourself from becoming distracted by the next shiny ball. When you do, you will find that your stress and anxiety is reduced and you are better able to focus on the opportunities that align with your goals. (For more on this, I recommend you read *When to Say Yes* by Don Khouri.)

Start with the creation of your buyer personae to document what you have learned about them so far. Write it all down, from their challenges and impacts to their communication styles and buying steps. Use the "**Buyer Persona Workbook Template**" in the **Buyer First Workbook**. Go further into how to build out buyer personae and value propositions with Lisa Dennis's book *Value Propositions That Sell* and with *Waiting for Your Cat to Bark?* by Bryan and Jeffrey Eisenberg.

You can't manage time, but you can prioritize it to align with your goals. When you have cue-based timelines for actions to take, you are more likely to reach your goals. Buy a new planner that aligns with how you think, or use the process I have described with a simple notebook and pencil.

The secret to scaling your business lies in your documents, processes, and systems first, and then in hiring the right people with the necessary mindsets and skill sets to grow sales. With the work you do on your own sales mindsets and behaviors, you will create a #buyerfirst culture and mindset for the sellers you hire and manage.

In doing the exercises in the Buyer First Workbook, you have started the process of aligning your focus and activities to your meaningful goals. You know what to do. You can do it. Repeat to yourself that selling isn't something you do *to* others, it is something you do *with* them. Continue the work of shifting to a #buyerfirst mindset to sell with your buyers. You have a plan, a support system, and—if you want—a coach.

Keep taking the steps to sell with your buyers, and you will change your world and theirs. Be the example.

"I've got this." Say it out loud.

Now go get it.

ACKNOWLEDGMENTS

THIS IS THE PART where I'm supposed to acknowledge everyone who helped bring this book into being.

And I'm a bit terrified, certain I will forget someone. For all the random things I remember in detail (my husband often calls me his little Rain Man), I often wonder why I walked into a room, what I was going to search for on Google, or why I put the silverware in the fridge.

Perhaps that's why I write, to try to catch the ideas and stories before they slip away, leaving me staring off into space, hoping they return.

The fact is, there are too many people to list who helped me birth this book. If it weren't for them, this book would not exist. It is from them as much as it is from me. Many I have mentioned or quoted in this book. For everyone else, please forgive this incomplete list.

Anyone who follows me online knows I share a lot about my family and is likely not surprised to see them mentioned throughout these pages. They are the ones who continue to hold me up throughout this whole messy process called entrepreneurship. Who fed me when I forgot to eat, made me laugh when I wanted to cry, and gave me the space I needed to focus when I was ready to pull my hair out. Who stood by and watched me labor as I birthed this book—you are a constant reminder of my "why." Without you—Steve, Nate, and MJ—this book could not exist. And my extended "family"—Cindy and the Snow clan—who sheltered me in SoFlo to save me from the sub-zero temps in Maine so I could finish my writing in sunshine.

This book is from my mom, who let me ride my bike alone to the library for summer reading contests, gave me my first journal to write all my crazy thoughts down, and tolerated my Edgar Allan Poe phase. And from my sister Heidi, who simply smiled and nodded without judgment when I said over and over, "I am going to finish my book."

This book is from Lori Richardson and my Women Sales Pros colleagues, whose support and introductions help me raise the bar, now and tomorrow.

The research that served as the foundation for this book is from Barbara Weaver Smith. Thank you for helping me get liftoff and encouraging me to challenge my own biases.

It is from AJ Harper, Laura Stone, and all my Top Three Book Workshop cohorts—especially those at the retreat. You, me, and Stephen King have that one secret place in common. Your feedback and encouragement against the trolls were my everlasting light in the cave.

From my advance readers—Adria Jefferies, Howard Tan, Laura Vaughan, Susie Perkowitz, and John Marrett—who saw the message through the messy first draft and were instrumental in the editing process.

From the team at Heroic Public Speaking: Michael and Amy Port, you made all of this work accessible and fun. I dream bigger today because of you. Sienna Roman—I love the way your brain works, and how you helped me bring it all together with a bow on top.

From the team at Objective Management Group—Rocky, Rick, John, Ryan, and Dave—your vision of sales as a science and your support in helping me analyze the data and coaching to help me change my own mindsets is what set me on this path.

From all my clients—whom I lovingly call my lab rats—that tested and tried these strategies in real life: thank you for your faith and trust in me to help you with your goals, fears, and challenges—I cannot wait to see what you do next.

From the team at Page Two—Trena, Adrineh, James, Peter, and Melissa—you were my labor coaches who kept me on deadline and talked me off the ledge a few times. You are the best.

Finally, this book is from Felicia Motel, Elysia Valdivia, and Lou Bortone—my magicians behind the scenes. Because of your support (when I often didn't know I needed it), I was able to dance when I stumbled and still looked good doing it.

SOURCES AND FURTHER READING

Achor, Shawn. *The Happiness Advantage: How a Positive Brain Fuels Success in Work and Life*. Currency, 2018.

Adamson, Brent, and Nick Toman. *5 Ways the Future of B2B Buying Will Rewrite the Rules of Effective Selling*. Gartner, August 4, 2020. emtemp.gcom.cloud/ngw/globalassets/en/sales-service/documents/trends/5-ways-the-future-of-b2b-buying.pdf

Allcott, Hunt, and Todd Rogers. "The Short-Run and Long-Run Effects of Behavioral Interventions: Experimental Evidence from Energy Conservation." *American Economic Review* 104, no. 10 (2014). doi.org/10.1257/aer.104.10.3003

Arabi, Shahida. "Do You Seek Validation from Others? Here's How to Stop." *Psych Central*, March 29, 2022. psychcentral.com/health/steps-to-stop-seeking-approval-from-others

Bonney, Leff. *The Problem with Personas: A Case Study for Segmentation That Sells*. B2B DecisionLabs. b2bdecisionlabs.com/research-center/report-the-problem-with-personas

Bounds, Gwendolyn. "How Handwriting Trains the Brain." *Wall Street Journal*, October 5, 2010. wsj.com/articles/SB10001424052748704631504575531932754922518

Bronée, Jeanette. *The Self-Care Mindset: Rethinking How We Change and Grow, Harness Well-Being, and Reclaim Work-Life Quality*. Wiley, 2022.

Burke, Lora, Jing Wang, and Mary Ann Sevick. "Self-Monitoring in Weight Loss: A Systematic Review of the Literature." *Journal of the American Academy of Nutrition and Dietetics* 111, no. 1 (2011). doi.org/10.1016/j.jada.2010.10.008

Carey, Michael P., and Andrew D. Forsyth. "Teaching Tip Sheet: Self-Efficacy." Public Interest Directorate, American Psychological Association, 2009. apa.org/pi/aids/resources/education/self-efficacy

Carnegie, Dale. *How to Win Friends and Influence People*. Updated edition. Gallery Books, 2022.

Carrell, Scott, Richard Fullerton, and James West. "Does Your Cohort Matter? Measuring Peer Effects in College Achievement." *Journal of Labor Economics* 27, no. 3 (2009). doi.org/10.1086/600143

Carter, Timothy. "The True Failure Rate of Small Businesses." *Entrepreneur*, January 3, 2021. entrepreneur.com/starting-a-business/the-true-failure-rate-of-small-businesses/361350

Cespedes, Frank, and Yuchun Lee. "Your Sales Training Is Probably Lackluster. Here's How to Fix It." *Harvard Business Review*, June 12, 2017. hbr.org/2017/06/your-sales-training-is-probably-lackluster-heres-how-to-fix-it

Chamorro-Premuzic, Tomas. "How to Become a Better Listener, According to Science." *Fast Company*, May 6, 2022. fastcompany.com/90749446/how-to-become-a-better-listener-according-to-science

Chamorro-Premuzic, Tomas. *Why Do So Many Incompetent Men Become Leaders? (And How to Fix It)*. Harvard Business Review Press, 2019.

Chen, Frances, Julia Minson, and Zakary Tormala. "Tell Me More: The Effects of Expressed Interest on Receptiveness during Dialog." *Journal of Experimental Social Psychology* 46, no. 5 (2010). doi.org/10.1016/j.jesp.2010.04.012

Clear, James. *Atomic Habits: An Easy & Proven Way to Build Good Habits & Break Bad Ones*. Penguin, 2018.

CSO Insights. *Fifth Annual Sales Enablement Study*. Miller Heiman Group, 2019. salesenablement.pro/assets/2019/10/CSO-Insights-5th-Annual-Sales-Enablement-Study.pdf

Damon, William. "Purpose and the Life Review." *Psychology Today*, July 28, 2021. psychologytoday.com/us/blog/the-puzzles-your-past/202107/purpose-and-the-life-review

Davis, Tchiki. "How to Control Your Emotions When They Are Out of Control." *Psychology Today*, October 1, 2018. psychologytoday.com/us/blog/click-here-happiness/201810/how-control-your-emotions-when-they-are-out-control

Dennis, Lisa D. *Value Propositions That Sell: Turning Your Message Into a Magnet That Attracts Buyers*. Mind Your Business Press, 2018.

Dreeke, Robin, and Cameron Stauth. *The Code of Trust: An American Counterintelligence Expert's Five Rules to Lead and Succeed.* St. Martin's Press, 2017.

Dweck, Carol. *Mindset: The New Psychology of Success*. Ballantine, 2007.

Eisenberg, Bryan, and Jeffrey Eisenberg, with Lisa T. Davis. *Waiting for Your Cat to Bark? Persuading Customers When They Ignore Marketing*. HarperCollins, 2007.

Ericsson, Anders, and Robert Pool. *Peak: Secrets from the New Science of Expertise*. HarperOne, 2017.

Eskreis-Winkler, Lauren, Katherine Milkman, Dena Gromet, and Angela Duckworth. "A Large-Scale Field Experiment Shows Giving Advice Improves Academic Outcomes for the Advisor." *Proceedings of the National Academy of Sciences* 116, no. 30 (2019). doi.org/10.1073/pnas.1908779116

Ewing Marion Kauffman Foundation. "Fewer New Businesses Have Become Employers." *Trends in Entrepreneurship*, no. 11 (2020). kauffman.org/wp-content/uploads/2020/07/Kauffman_Trends-in-Entrepreneurship-11-Fewer-New-Businesses-Have-Become-Employers-2005-2019_2020.pdf

Fenton, Richard, and Andrea Waltz. *Go for No! Yes Is the Destination. No Is How You Get There.* Courage Crafters, 2010.

Fishbein, Martin, and Icek Ajzen. *Belief, Attitude, Intention and Behavior: An Introduction to Theory and Research*. Addison-Wesley, 1975.

Gollwitzer, Peter, and Veronika Brandstätter. "Implementation Intentions and Effective Goal Pursuit." *Journal of Personality and Social Psychology* 73, no. 1 (1997). doi.org/10.1037/0022-3514.73.1.186

Hafenbrack, Andrew, Zoe Kinias, and Sigal Barsade. "Debiasing the Mind through Meditation: Mindfulness and the Sunk-Cost Bias." *Psychological Science* 25, no. 2 (2013). doi.org/10.1177/0956797613503853

Hansen, Julie. *Act Like a Sales Pro: How to Command the Business Stage and Dramatically Increase Your Sales with Proven Acting Techniques.* Career Press, 2011.

Harper, AJ. *Write a Must-Read: Craft a Book That Changes Lives—Including Your Own*. Page Two, 2022.

Heiman, Liz. Interview with author, May 4, 2022.

Highfill, Tina, Richard Cao, Richard Schwinn, Richard Prisinzano, and Danny Leung. "Measuring the Small Business Economy." U.S. Bureau of Economic Analysis, Working Paper Series WP2020-4, March 2020. bea.gov/system/files/papers/BEA-WP2020-4_0.pdf

Hoffeld, David. *The Science of Selling: Proven Strategies to Make Your Pitch, Influence Decisions, and Close the Deal.* TarcherPerigee, 2016.

Hölzel, Britta, James Carmody, Mark Vangel, Christina Congleton, Sita Yerramsetti, Tim Gard, and Sara Lazar. "Mindfulness Practice Leads to Increases in Regional Brain Gray Matter Density." *Psychiatry Research: Neuroimaging* 191, no. 1 (2011). doi.org/10.1016/j.pscychresns.2010.08.006

Hutton, Doug, Tim Riesterer, Nick Lee, and Carmen Simon. *Avoid the Parity Trap: Differentiating Your Solutions in Highly Competitive Categories.* B2B DecisionLabs. b2bdecisionlabs.com/research-center/report-differentiating-your-solutions-in-highly-competitive-categories

Iconomopoulos, Fotini. *Say Less, Get More: Unconventional Negotiation Techniques to Get What You Want.* Collins, 2021.

James, Karin Harman. "Sensori-Motor Experience Leads to Changes in Visual Processing in the Developing Brain." *Developmental Science* 13, no. 2 (2010). doi.org/10.1111/j.1467-7687.2009.00883.x

Jones, Alison. "For a Modest Personality Trait, 'Intellectual Humility' Packs a Punch!" *Duke Today*, March 7, 2017. today.duke.edu/2017/03/modest-personality-trait-intellectual-humility-packs-punch

Judge, Timothy, Ronald Piccolo, Nathan Podsakoff, John Shaw, and Bruce Rich. "The Relationship between Pay and Job Satisfaction: A Meta-Analysis of the Literature." *Journal of Vocational Behavior* 77, no. 2 (2010). doi.org/10.1016/j.jvb.2010.04.002

Khouri, Don. *When to Say Yes: The 5 Steps to Protect Your Time.* Page Two, 2021.

Kobayashi, Keiichi. "Interactivity: A Potential Determinant of Learning by Preparing to Teach and Teaching." *Frontiers in Psychology* 9 (2018). doi.org/10.3389/fpsyg.2018.02755

Kouzes, James, Barry Posner, and Deb Calvert. *Stop Selling & Start Leading: How to Make Extraordinary Sales Happen.* Wiley, 2018.

Kurlan, Dave. *Baseline Selling: How to Become a Sales Superstar by Using What You Already Know about the Game of Baseball.* AuthorHouse, 2006.

Kurlan, Dave. "New Analysis Shows the 5 Biggest Gaps between Top and Bottom Sales Performers." *Understanding the Sales Force,*

Objective Management Group, May 1, 2017. https://www.omghub.com/salesdevelopmentblog/new-analysis-shows-the-5-biggest-gaps-between-top-and-bottom-sales-performers

Kurlan, Dave. "New Data Shows Sales Weaknesses Cause Powerful Chain Reactions in Salespeople." *Understanding the Sales Force*, Objective Management Group, May 30, 2018. https://www.omghub.com/salesdevelopmentblog/new-data-shows-sales-weaknesses-cause-powerful-chain-reactions-in-salespeople

Leahy, Robert L. "Ten Steps to Overcoming Need for Approval." *Psychology Today*, June 12, 2017. psychologytoday.com/us/blog/anxiety-files/201706/ten-steps-overcoming-need-approval

Leary, Mark, Kate Diebels, Erin Davisson, Katrina Jongman-Sereno, Jennifer Isherwood, Kaitlin Raimi, Samantha Deffler, and Rick Hoyle. "Cognitive and Interpersonal Features of Intellectual Humility." *Personality and Social Psychology Bulletin* 43, no. 6 (2017). doi.org/10.1177/0146167217697695

LinkedIn Sales Solutions. *Buyer First: A New Era in Selling* (2020). business.linkedin.com/content/dam/me/business/en-us/sales-solutions/products/pdfs/LinkedIn-Sales-Solutions-October-2020-Buyer-First.pdf

LinkedIn Sales Solutions. *The LinkedIn State of Sales Report 2020: United States Edition*. business.linkedin.com/sales-solutions/b2b-sales-strategy-guides/the-state-of-sales-2020-report

LinkedIn Sales Solutions. *The State of Sales Report 2021: United States & Canada Edition*. business.linkedin.com/sales-solutions/b2b-sales-strategy-guides/the-state-of-sales-2021-report

Lussier, Bruno, Yany Grégoire, and Marc-Antoine Vachon. "The Role of Humor Usage on Creativity, Trust and Performance in Business Relationships: An Analysis of the Salesperson-Customer Dyad." *Industrial Marketing Management* 65 (2017). doi.org/10.1016/j.indmarman.2017.03.012

Manson, Mark. *The Subtle Art of Not Giving a F*ck: A Counterintuitive Approach to Living a Good Life*. Harper, 2016.

McCormack, Mark H. *What They Don't Teach You at Harvard Business School: Notes from a Street-Smart Executive*. Bantam, 1986.

Mehr, Katie, Amanda Geiser, Katherine Milkman, and Angela Duckworth. "Copy-Paste Prompts: A New Nudge to Promote Goal Achievement." *Journal of the Association for Consumer Research* 5, no. 3 (2020). doi.org/10.1086/708880

Milkman, Katy. *How to Change: The Science of Getting from Where You Are to Where You Want to Be*. Penguin, 2021.

Murayama, Kou. "The Science of Motivation." *Psychological Science Agenda*, American Psychological Association, June 2018. apa.org/science/about/psa/2018/06/motivation

Murphy, Karen, and Olivia Creux. "Examining the Association between Media Multitasking, and Performance on Working Memory and Inhibition Tasks." *Computers in Human Behavior* 114 (2021). doi.org/10.1016/j.chb.2020.106532

Norton, Michael, Daniel Mochon, and Dan Ariely. "The IKEA Effect: When Labor Leads to Love." *Journal of Consumer Psychology* 22, no. 3 (2012). doi.org/10.1016/j.jcps.2011.08.002

Objective Management Group. "Explore Our Sales Statistics, and See How Your Salespeople Compare for Free." stats.objectivemanagement.com

Onyemah, Vincent, Martha Rivera Pesquera, and Abdul Ali. "What Entrepreneurs Get Wrong." *Harvard Business Review*, May 2013. hbr.org/2013/05/what-entrepreneurs-get-wrong

Orlob, Chris. "The 11 Best Discovery Call Tips for Sales You'll Read This Year." Gong, March 28, 2019. gong.io/blog/best-discovery-call-tips

Parker, Clifton. "Sense of Youthful Purpose Driven by Action, Passion, Says Stanford Researcher." *Stanford News*, April 14, 2015. news.stanford.edu/2015/04/14/purpose-youth-damon-041415

Pink, Daniel H. *To Sell Is Human: The Surprising Truth about Moving Others*. Penguin, 2013.

Port, Michael. *Steal the Show: From Speeches to Job Interviews to Deal-Closing Pitches, How to Guarantee a Standing Ovation for All the Performances in Your Life*. Mariner Books, 2015.

"The Power of the Placebo Effect." Harvard Health Publishing, December 13, 2021. health.harvard.edu/mental-health/the-power-of-the-placebo-effect

Psychology Today. "Perfectionism." psychologytoday.com/us/basics/perfectionism

Riesterer, Tim, Erik Peterson, and Zakary Tormala. "Where Do Questions Fit Into an Insight Selling Model?" B2B DecisionLabs. b2bdecisionlabs.com/research-center/research-brief-the-effect-of-leading-with-insights

Riesterer, Tim, Rob Perrilleon, and Nick Lee. *The Key to the C-Suite: Messaging for Executive Access*. B2B DecisionLabs. b2bdecisionlabs.com/research-center/report-key-to-the-c-suite-messaging-for-executive-access

Roberge, Mark. *The Sales Acceleration Formula: Using Data, Technology, and Inbound Selling to Go from $0 to $100 Million*. Wiley, 2015.

Schmitt, Philipp, Bernd Skiera, and Christophe Van den Bulte. "Do Referral Programs Increase Profits?" *Marketing Intelligence Review* 5, no. 1 (2013). doi.org/10.2478/gfkmir-2014-0020

Sharot, Tali, Alison Riccardi, Candace Raio, and Elizabeth Phelps. "Neural Mechanisms Mediating Optimism Bias." *Nature* 450, no. 7166 (2007). doi.org/10.1038/nature06280

Tamir, Diana, and Jason Mitchell. "Disclosing Information about the Self Is Intrinsically Rewarding." *Proceedings of the National Academy of Sciences* 109, no. 21 (2012). doi.org/10.1073/pnas.1202129109

Technical University of Munich. "Harnessing ADHD for Business Success: Attention Deficit Hyperactivity Disorder (ADHD) Promotes Entrepreneurial Skills." *ScienceDaily*, March 9, 2017. sciencedaily.com/releases/2017/03/170309132303.htm

Thaler, Richard H. *Misbehaving: The Making of Behavioral Economics*. W.W. Norton, 2016.

Zak, Paul J. "The Trust Molecule." *Wall Street Journal*, April 27, 2012. wsj.com/articles/SB10001424052702304811304577365782995320366

ABOUT THE AUTHOR

CAROLE MAHONEY is a sales coach for the Entrepreneurial MBA program at Harvard Business School, where she's been called "the Sales Therapist." She has been named a top sales influencer by LinkedIn, a top sales coach by Ambition, and a sales leader to watch by Sales Hacker. She is the president of the Boston Chapter of the American Association of Inside Sales Professionals. As the founder of consulting agency Unbound Growth, Mahoney draws on cutting-edge science, statistics, and data from 2.2 million sales professionals to inform her sales coaching work with clients. She holds a BA in marketing and business management from Franklin Pierce University. She lives in Maine.